FROM BEYOND THE VEIL

Manifestations at the Crossroads of Heaven and Earth

FROM BEYOND THE VEIL
Manifestations at the Crossroads of Heaven and Earth

JASON EARL SIGNOR

A Spiritual Memoir

JAHbookdesign | York, PA

From Beyond the Veil is a work of nonfiction. However, the names of some individuals have been changed to disguise their identities. Any resulting resemblance to persons living or dead is entirely coincidental and unintentional.

Copyright © 2020 by Jason E. Signor. All rights reserved.
Imprint: Independently published
Printed in the United States of America
ISBN: 9798679593961

Scripture quotations marked AMP are from the *Amplified*(R) *Bible*, Copyright © 2015 by The Lockman Foundation. Used by permission. lockman.org.

Scripture quotations marked AMPC are from the *Amplified*(R) *Bible*, Classic Edition, Copyright © 1954, 1958, 1962, 1964, 1965, 1987 by The Lockman Foundation. Used by permission. lockman.org.

Scripture quotations marked DBY are from the *Darby Bible*, 1890, by John Nelson Darby. Public domain. biblegateway.com/versions/Darby-Translation-Bible.

Scripture quotations marked ERV are from *The Holy Bible: Easy-To-Read Version*, Copyright © 2014 by Bible League International. Used by permission. bibleleague.org.

Scripture quotations marked NIV are from *The Holy Bible, New International Version*(R), NIV(R), Copyright © 1973, 1978, 1984, 2011 by Biblica, Inc.(R). Used by permission. All rights reserved worldwide. *New International Version*(R), and NIV(R), are registered trademarks of Biblica, Inc. Use of these trademarks for offering goods or services requires consent of Biblica US, Inc. biblica.com.

Scripture quotations marked NLV are from the *New Life Version*™, Copyright © 1969, 2003 by Barbour Publishing, Inc. Used by Permission. barbourbooks.com.

Scripture quotations marked TPT are from *The Passion Translation*(R), Copyright © 2017, 2018 by Passion & Fire Ministries, Inc. Used by permission. All rights reserved. thepassiontranslation.com.

Scripture quotations marked VOICE are from *The Voice*™, Copyright © 2012 by Ecclesia Bible Society. *The Voice*™ translation, Copyright © 2012, Thomas Nelson, Inc. Used by permission. All rights reserved. thomasnelson.com.

Scripture quotations marked WEB are from the *World English Bible*. The name *World English Bible* is trademarked. Public Domain. worldenglish.bible.

Cover designer and editor: Joshua Holmes | JAHbookdesign.com

To God – for loving me, healing me, filling me, and giving me hope and purpose.

To my parents, Gene and Sharon Signor – who taught me to love.

To my twin brother, Aaron – my best friend in all of life.

*To all who listen –
May they hear the Voice of Love.
To all who thirst –
May they drink freely from the Fountain of Living Water.
To all who hunger –
May they eat the Bread of Life and never grow hungry.
To all who are blind –
May they see.
To all who suffer –
May they find lasting peace.*

*With Love,
Jason*

CONTENTS

PREFACE ix
ACKNOWLEDGMENTS xvii
PART ONE | THE VOICE 3
1. LOST IN SOLON 5
    A Lesson 16
2. UNEXPECTED GRACE 21
    Fear and Peace 37
3. THE MANIFEST PRESENCE 39
    Suffering and Grace 43
4. DESERT AWAKENING 49
    More Than Words 71
5. A NEW HOME 81
    Looking Ahead and Back 95
6. SUNDAY NIGHT VOICES 103
    An Open Heart 109
7. EXTERNAL VOICES 115
    Lighten the Burdens 119
8. NO ORDINARY CAT 125
    Spontaneous Selflessness 133
PART TWO | THE ANGELIC 143

9. THE LENS 145
   Sight 149
10. AMTRAK ANGEL 157
   Shelter 169
11. INFORMATION PLEASE! 173
   Sustenance 177
12. SILENCE! 183
   Peace 189
13. BUTTER ANGEL 197
   Joy 201
   Communion 204
14. DRUNK IN THE PARK 207
   Humility 210
15. BIG MONEY 219
   Blessing and Abundance 222
16. WHEN YOU FALL 231
   Hope 238
APPENDIX 243
NOTES 245
ABOUT THE AUTHOR 267
ABOUT THE TYPE 269
ABOUT THE COVER 271
LET'S CONNECT! 273

PREFACE

CONSIDERING THE MANY ways I can introduce a book about my spiritual journey, there's probably none better than to tell you about my family. After all, our families are the primary gristmill for moral and spiritual development. Of course, there are other avenues that come along as we grow, but family is where it starts.

First, a bit about human development and about this book.

Some parents nurture well, creating bonds of secure attachment between themselves and their children. These children flourish. They feel safe and they know they're loved. Other children are not so fortunate. Far too many children are victims of abuse and neglect.

But whether our families were loving, dysfunctional, or somewhere in-between, we usually learn a combination of helpful and unhelpful beliefs. Some of these persist throughout the generations. As we grow, we learn to question our beliefs. We keep some and discard others.

And regardless of how we're raised, our Heavenly Father stands with arms wide open, ready to provide the love we didn't receive—to whatever degree—from our families or elsewhere.

We have direct access to God. The temple veil is torn.[1] To connect with God, all we need to do is reach out with our hearts, acknowledge our sinfulness, and our need for Him! And let love and forgiveness fill us! *That's how it begins!*

My primary intentions for this book are: (1) to show the reader that a real, living, personal relationship with God is possible—one where we know, hear, feel, and see the Divine in our daily lives; (2) to emphasize the importance—and power—of love in relationships and community.

To be clear, this book is not meant to show I am some spiritual superhero. I'm not. Nor is my journey neat and complete. It's not! You'll read about my spiritual endeavors, including times I've struggled. For sure, my life is a continual process of healing and growth.

So, in addition to the two main intentions I've stated above, I hope my reads can see—like I have—that spiritual growth is a lifelong process. A journey.

To best convey this message, I've chosen to section the book into two parts.

Part One, entitled *The Voice*, focuses on the various ways God communicates with us. I've chosen unique names for each: The Inner Voice, Unexpected Grace, The Manifest Presence, The Visual Voice, and The External Voice. The Divine Cinematographer and The Divine Script represent communication in dreams. And you'll read about the value of community. Each chapter in Part One conveys one or more of these modes, within the context of a true story from my life. Following each of the eight stories is life lesson.

Part Two, entitled *The Angelic*, reveals my personal encounters with angels. I encourage you to suspend doubt and open your heart as you read, and to open your heart to God's messengers in your own life. All eight chapters in Part Two tell

PREFACE

real stories from my life. And, as with Part One, a unique lesson follows each.

I've told the stories—sixteen in total—exactly as they happened. While I've chosen pseudonyms to represent most of the real-life characters, I've kept the actual names of individuals who've greatly impacted me.

This book is best read in order, from front to back. Part One is ordered chronologically. Part Two is also ordered chronologically. But both Part One and Part Two together, overlap in time. So, for your reference, I've provided a chronological list of all sixteen chapters in the Appendix.

You'll notice breaks through the body text. One kind is shown below—a squiggle. This symbolizes a forward-moving break in time, or the start of a new topic or subtopic. The second kind of break, you'll see at the beginning and ending of flashbacks. For these sections I've used three bold dots to show their beginning and ending. At times you will see two flashbacks presented simultaneously.

Also, in addition to the standard practice of writing dialogue within quotation marks and internal thoughts in italics, you'll see two other dialogue formats used throughout the book.

Bold, italicized dialogue represents God's communication to me internally.

"Bold, italicized dialogue in quotation marks" shows God speaking audibly— e.g. through a person, an angel, or directly to me in a dream.

⦈⦇

And now, what you've waited for. About my family.

A MESSAGE IN TIME

When my twin brother and I were young, Mom read to us frequently. In fact, I recall her reading to us every night for many years. She prepared fruit slices as our nighttime snack, then we sat on either side of her as she read to us. We read many stories. Some were especially memorable. (It's no surprise to me she pursued a career as an elementary school teacher).

I recall *Timothy's Forest* by Freya and Harold Littledale.[2] Timothy lived in the city where there was no forest, so he created one in his bedroom. The story engaged my creative mind at a young age. My brother, Aaron, and I enjoyed the story so much we asked to hear it repeatedly.

Then there was C. S. Lewis's *The Chronicles of Narnia*.[3] I loved the thought of traveling to other worlds through multiple pools; that something impossible in ordinary experience was plausible in imagination—and therefore *might actually be possible!* The story engaged my spiritual curiosity early on in my life.

And I recall a story by social worker Richard Lessor about a valley community who shared little creatures called *fuzzies*. The people were happy until Juanita, the head witch of the Blahs, convinced them to stop giving. The people turned selfish and cold. They hoarded the fuzzies and locked them away until they withered for lack of love and sustenance. The people forgot about them, except for one woman. She wondered what life would've been like had there never been a shortage of fuzzies. Lessor's story, *Fuzzies: A Folk Fable for All Ages*,[4] taught me the joy of sharing and the consequences of greed.

PREFACE

And I recall a story that described God as Spirit. I asked Mom, "What does it mean that God is a Spirit?" And she said, "It means even though you can't see him, he's there!" A circle of swirling colors filled the book's page, indicating God's presence. And from that night forward I envisioned God as Spirit. I never held the image of God as an unkind old man, ready to dish out punishment at any time, like some kids did. The image permanently shaped my view of God.

These three themes—*creativity*, God as *Spirit* (rather than religion), and *giving and sharing*—stayed with me. They impacted my childhood, my career choices, and my relationships. And you'll recognize them in this book. Creativity, spirituality, and giving go together!

My parents instilled in me a strong work ethic. And they led by example. Dad worked nonstop for forty years as a college administrator. Mom taught kindergarten, first, and second grade for many years. And they've stayed active and healthy in their retirement years.

As my parents' careers were in educational institutions, it's not surprising to me I've spent much of my life in the same, completing a bachelor's degree, two master's degrees, and five other training programs.

Through excellent instruction in high school and ample opportunities in my college years, I learned to write! Some of the writing was creative, but most of it was research-based. It wasn't until recently, however, I learned creative writing well enough to produce an entire book. For that, I thank my good friend Joshua Holmes, who taught me.

A MESSAGE IN TIME

You'll see my diligence in this book's pages. And the theme of *continuous personal and spiritual growth*. I believe our lives are best lived when we continue to learn and grow. When we stop learning and growing, we fade. Why stop when there are endless opportunities to learn and share our gifts with the world?

My identical twin brother, Aaron, and I share much in common. We think alike, we share many of the same joys and difficulties, we both have *albinism* and *low vision*.[5] We're not just brothers; we're best friends.

I can only imagine what it would've been like growing up in the 1970s and '80s without him. I truly feel for all kids with disabilities who lack a supportive parent or sibling. I consider it a great blessing to journey through this life with Aaron. As you read, remember this. You'll hear a lot from Aaron.

And know that my spiritual journey and experience of disability coincide. They also complement each other. Living with albinism and low vision has strengthened me spiritually. And knowing God personally has helped me accept myself.

Though growing up with albinism and low vision was difficult, I've increasingly acknowledged them as tremendous sources of learning and strength, rather than weakness. I've learned I can find hope, not only in comfort and peace, but also through hardship.

The theme of *hope* runs through the entire book. You will see this in my experiences and others'.

PREFACE

I grew up going to church. But I didn't know God personally. In adolescence, however, two spiritual experiences sparked my curiosity—and from then forward it grew. I desired to know the One who spoke to me.

While I've omitted one of these stories from this book, the other begins *your* journey through *my* journey—in chapter 1.

You'll be glad it's a survival story. I can't really ask for a better way to start a book!

Wintry Central New York.

A *bad* environment for getting lost skiing!

But that's what happened to me at age twelve.

God spoke to me.

I dismissed it.

And I learned a valuable lesson.

The first of *many* lessons!

—JASON SIGNOR

ACKNOWLEDGMENTS

FIRST AND FOREMOST, thank you **God**, for all the ways you meet me, heal me, and give me hope—through Jesus's sacrifice, through your *still small voice*,[1] your amazing grace, your manifest presence, the kindness of others, through prophetic dreams, through encounters with angels, and all the other myriad ways you show your love. Thank you for giving me the inspiration, patience, and strength to complete this book and offer it to the world.

Joshua Holmes: I thank my good friend Joshua Holmes for teaching me creative writing, and for editing this book and designing its cover. Thank you for your knowledge, patience, creativity, and commitment to helping make *From Beyond the Veil* a reality.

Grateful acknowledgement is made to the following for permission to reprint previously published material:

Barbour Publishing: Scripture quotations taken from *The Holy Bible, New Life Version (NLV)*, Copyright © 1969, 2003. Used by Permission of Barbour Publishing, Inc., Uhrichsville, OH, USA. https://www.barbourbooks.com.

Grand Central Publishing: Excerpt from *Touched by Angels: True Cases of Close Encounters of the Celestial Kind* by Eileen Elias

Freeman, Copyright © 1994. Reprinted by permission of Grand Central Publishing, an imprint of Hachette Book Group, Inc., New York, NY, USA. https://www.grandcentralpublishing.com.

Hatch: Excerpt by Roanne van Voorst, from "The Flipside of Fear: Freedom & Desire," online course module 1.4, *Courage Building & Personal Leadership*, Copyright © 2019. Used by permission of Hatch, Amsterdam, North Holland, NLD. https://www.iamhatch.com.

Hay House Publishing: Excerpt from *Inspiration Deficit Disorder* by Jonathan H. Ellerby, Copyright © 2010. Used by permission of Hay House Publishing, Carlsbad, CA, USA. https://www.hayhouse.com.

The MIT Press: Excerpt from *The Character of Physical Law* by Richard Feyman, Copyright © 1965; repr., Cambridge: The MIT Press, 2017. Used by permission of The MIT Press. https://mitpress.mit.edu.

Wm. B. Eerdmans Publishing Company: Excerpt from *A Theology of the New Testament* by George Eldon Ladd, Copyright © 1974. Used by permission of Wm. B. Eerdmans Publishing Company, Grand Rapids, MI, USA. https://www.eerdmans.com.

Zondervan: Paraphrase of the story of Hien Pham, taken from *Walking from East to West: God in the Shadows* by Ravi Zacharias and R. S. B. Sawyer, Copyright © 2006. Used by permission of Zondervan, Grand Rapids, MI, USA. https://www.zondervan.com.

FROM BEYOND THE VEIL
Manifestations at the Crossroads of Heaven and Earth

PART ONE | THE VOICE

1. LOST IN SOLON

Intuition is more than the accumulation of old information in an instantaneous brain blast. It's the gut feeling, the hunch, or "knowing" that defies experience or understanding.

—Jonathan H. Ellerby [1]

IT WAS THE middle of winter, 1985. The church ski trip sounded like a fun break from the routine of seventh grade. It was a sunny but cold Saturday, the ground full of snow, the skies cloudless and blue. Perfect conditions for an afternoon of cross-country skiing. I was unaware, however, that it would quickly turn into one of the scariest experiences of my life and a profound life lesson.

Early in the afternoon, we headed to Solon, ten miles east of my childhood home in Cortland, New York. Our group parked at the intersection of Telephone and Kiwanis Roads on the southwest corner of the vast Taylor Valley State Forest—an uninhabited 4,638 acres of wilderness, popular for family recreational activities such as skiing, snowmobiling, hunting, hiking, and camping.

When Mom and I arrived, there were few people around. Most of the group was already skiing, including Dad and my twin brother, Aaron. There was no traffic, and the snow muffled our voices.

"Go ahead," said Mom.

"Are you sure?" I said.

"Yeah," she said. "I'll be right there."

"Okay. But I'm not sure where to go."

I turned and looked for a trail. I wasn't sure where to start as I made my way over to the woods' edge.

Wait. Something's not right. I don't see anyone else.

I headed back to the station wagon.

"I'll wait," I said.

"Don't be silly," said Mom, now at the back of the car getting her skis. "Go ahead."

"Alright," I said, turning once again to face the vast, unknown forest, preparing to find a trail.

Go back!

An internal nudge. The Inner Voice.

1 | LOST IN SOLON

I stood for a moment, curious and unsettled. And again, I skied back to the car.

"I really don't think I should go ahead," I said. "What are you doing!?"

"I'm coming!" said Mom. "You can go ahead. Don't worry about it. Just follow everyone else."

By then, I muted The Inner Voice, much like the snow quieted our spoken words.

I found an entrance and began climbing a thirty-degree, upward slope into the hollow woods. A few minutes passed, and then I met the Mean Couple. They were not a part of our group. I knew that for sure.

"Your group went that way!" yelled the Mean Lady as she stood next to her silent partner. "You can do what you want, but I think you should go back!"

Why is she yelling?

I kept going.

Then, Andy, also my age, and in the same Sunday school class, suddenly skied up behind me.

"Is this the way we're supposed to go?" he said.

I paused and stared at the sky. "I'm not sure. I think so."

"They pointed me this way too," he said.

We continued on the narrow trail surrounded by looming, snow-caked evergreens. Eventually, we came to an area with tall, barren trees and a less-defined path.

Should we go back?

We encountered a small creek. I wondered whether it was liquid or frozen. Hard to tell, as it was snow-covered. Even in sunlight the air was bone-chilling; I knew we couldn't afford to get wet.

Maybe we should go back!

We successfully crossed the creek. And after several turns of the trail, the woods thickened and darkened like Caspar David Friedrich's *The Chasseur in the Forest*.

Then, the trail widened, and an opportunity emerged. There before us spanned a steep, downward slope, a thick canopy of snow-laden branches covering its entirety.

"I'm going for it!" said Andy.

"Now!? Don't you think we should find our way back!?"

My heart rate quickened.

"You don't have to, but I'm going," said Andy.

I watched in disbelief as he sped down the slope, disappearing around the curve.

Why aren't we staying together?

I paused. It was silent except for my heartbeat.

I'm going too. I don't want to be alone out here!

Bending my knees, I launched myself forward with enough speed to crash and break a leg. And for a while, I dismissed my fear, enjoying the curves.

Maybe this is not so bad after all.

The road twisted, continuing in its steepness without relent. Ten minutes passed before I reached the bottom.

∞

I arrived a few minutes after Andy. A clearing. It was brighter too.

That was steep and long! But was it worth it?

1 | LOST IN SOLON

I could see Andy, a speck in the distance. I caught up with him as we skied through the valley with its sparsely scattered evergreens.

We heard voices ahead of us and quickened our pace to identify their source.

"Do you know how to get back to the main trail?" I said. Suddenly, I realized we again encountered the Mean Couple.

"I tried to tell you!" yelled the Mean Lady, her partner silently propped on his ski poles next to her. "I'm not going to tell you again! I'm not going to show you, but you gotta go back the way you just came!"

I finally got the message. We were lost.

We're lost. And they're not going to help us!

I looked at Andy. We said nothing to each other as we skied back to the bottom of the slope.

I removed my frozen gloves, and reaching into my pocket, I found the plastic bag of carrot sticks Mom gave me. I felt a strange sense of nostalgia.

Will we make it out alive?

"Here!" I said, offering two carrot sticks to Andy and stuffing two in my mouth.

It sure is cold without gloves!

"Oh, that's probably a good idea," said Andy. "Thanks!"

"We'll need to climb back to the top. But I don't know if we can do it without skis."

I wonder if we have enough energy left!

I took off my right ski and tested the snow. My leg sank up to the knee and my heart sank just as far.

"We'll have to do this with skis on. And it's not going to be easy," I said, fear clawing at my throat.

"Well. We better get going," said Andy. "We don't have a choice."

The uphill climb exhausted me. Now I was both tired *and* cold. I didn't know what Andy felt, but I was angry with him for leading us astray.

We emerged at the top.

"Okay. Which way is the way back?" I said.

"Well, I think she said that way!" Andy pointed his ski pole.

"Who?"

"The woman. I talked to her before you got there."

"Oh, okay. But we came from *that* way!" I said, pointing straight ahead of me. "I'm going *that* way."

"Okay. Well, I'm going *this* way," he said.

We parted ways.

What are we doing!?

I knew we should have stayed together. But, but I no longer trusted Andy's judgment.

Exhausted, I made my way back to the trail we previously traversed. Five minutes in, confusion enveloped me. There was no evidence of the trail. I could have been anywhere in that 4,638 acres of wilderness.

What happened? Am I in the wrong place!?
This is not good. I'm really getting cold now.
Freezing!

Suddenly I felt a twinge of panic. Now, I was lost *and* alone.

How much time has passed?
An hour?
Two hours?
Three?

1 | LOST IN SOLON

Is the temperature diving?

The sun faded, time escaped me, and the frigid air penetrated my layers.

Ruminations. Disjointed thoughts.

It was too cold to think!

I felt like Jack London's main character in the perilous story, *To Build a Fire*. A newcomer, wholly unprepared for the severity of the situation. That scared me even more. And these were the days before cell phones and GPS!

I followed larger trails, hoping to find my way back to safety. Then, I arrived at a crossing—a broad road with snowmobile tracks beneath a snow layer.

I paused.

How much longer can I stay out here?

My feet are cold.

What if I'm here all night!?

Will I need to build a fire?

Can I build a fire myself?

I wondered which way I should go, knowing my choice would be critical to my survival.

I will pray and ask for help!

Never had I prayed so intensely.

God, please help me get back safely!

Draw an arrow in the snow.

Whichever way I point this, I trust that's the way.

Grabbing a branch, I stooped and inscribed a right-facing arrow. I imagined someone would see it and find me.

Silly thought. I'm surviving on prayer alone!

I descended the gradual slope and saw nothing but a mass of white powder.

Nothing!

Just the sound of my breath, the swishing of my skis, and the painful cold that gnawed at my ears.

Still nothing.

Time evaporated in the thin, evening air as I shut my eyes. I imagined a different place and time. I wasn't lost. A fun, relaxing day. Like this was supposed to be.

I jerked my head up, returning to consciousness. The sun, slanting through the trees, reminded me evening was pending.

A tightness gripped my throat.

An object moved in the distance. Or was it just me that moved in relation to it?

What is that?

I squinted. And waited.

Another skier appeared to be out in this frigid cold.

Is that Dad's red jacket?

The skier quickened its pace and then stood before me.

"Where have you been!?" said Dad. "We've been looking all over for you! Reverend Rose has been praying we would find you."

"I got lost," I said, my body now weak.

"There's a whole team of people looking for you," he said, finally smiling.

"What about Andy? He was with me, but we went different directions."

"Oh, he got back a while ago," Dad said. "Alright. We need to get going. You have two options. You can go back with me,

1 | LOST IN SOLON

or you can go back with a forest ranger on a snowmobile. If you want to go back with him, we'll have to meet him. It's up to you."

"I guess I'll go back with him."

"Okay. Follow me!"

He turned to the direction I came from.

So, this is the right way!

After several minutes, we arrived at a clearing in the woods with a steep-angled expanse covered with snow.

"I wonder if that's rock!?" I yelled down to Dad, who already made his way around it on a softer surface.

"I don't know, but why don't you come around this way!?"

"No, I want to try it!" I said, feeling better now that I'd been found.

"Are you sure!? We really do need to get back!" he said.

"Yeah, I want to!"

I launched myself on the hard surface and sped to the bottom without a hitch.

That was fun!

Later, a frightening discovery caused me to question how I managed the descent without serious injury.

"Wow, you could do that!?" Dad said.

"Yeah! It was easy, actually."

We slid back into the thick woods.

After several minutes, a distant buzz penetrated the silence.

Braap, brapp

The distinct sound of a two-stroke engine rose on the snow-muffled air, increasing in volume—until a maroon snowmobile sat rumbling next to us. A forest ranger dressed all in black dismounted and walked toward us.

"Hello! I'm Kevin. Glad to see you!" he said. "Are you Jason?"

"Yup! That's me!"

"And who are you?" he said, looking at Dad.

"I'm his father. I've been looking for him too. Thank you for your help!"

"Well, that's my job," Kevin said. "Now, I can only take one. Are you okay by yourself, sir?"

"I know the way back," said Dad. "Go ahead, Jason."

"You'll need to hold your gear as we go," Kevin said.

I climbed on the snowmobile and wrapped my arms around my skis, poles, and the ranger.

"Okay, now hold on tight!" he said.

My twelve-year-old arms didn't reach completely around him, but I held on as best I could.

"Okay, I'll meet you when we get back," Dad said, his voice fading in the engine noise.

Acceleration.

Then some speed.

Then a lot of speed!

Tall, barren trees and evergreens whizzed by. We swerved left and right. And the distance Andy and I traveled amazed me. We really were lost!

Finally, we emerged at the bottom, and I thanked the ranger. Only a few cars remained at the intersection of Kiwanis and Telephone Roads.

1 | LOST IN SOLON

Maybe they'll all be upset I wasted their time. I better make it look bad, so they believe me.

I dropped my skis in the middle of the road and stammered to the station wagon to demonstrate the situation's gravity. Mom was inside.

"You dropped your skis, Jason. Go back and get them!"

Reluctantly, I retrieved my skis and returned to the car. I flopped into the passenger's seat and pulled the door shut, sealing out the unsafe winter.

"Where were you!?" Mom said. "We were really worried!"

"We got lost. I guess we didn't go the right way," I said, hesitating to elaborate. "What time is it?"

"Six thirty! You've been out there a while," she said. "I hope you don't have hypothermia!"

"I'm cold," I said, reaching for my frozen boots. "I can't feel anything!"

"What!?" said Mom, startled.

She removed my boots.

"Can you feel anything now!?"

"No! Nothing!"

"Geez!" Mom said, hurrying to start the car.

For the next five minutes she rubbed my frozen feet under the radiator.

Feeling came back slowly.

Tingling. Pain. More pain. More tingling.

Warmth!

How did I manage to speed down that rock face and the foolish, winding slope with frozen feet!?

"Okay, I can feel again. I think I'm okay."

"Are you sure!?"

"Yeah. I'm okay now."
It was dark. We drove home.

I sat on the hearth directly in front of our roaring fireplace, thawing and drinking hot chocolate. Mom and Dad sat nearby, and we talked. Aaron slept upstairs.

"Well, just be glad we were able to find you!" Mom said.

"Yeah, that's for sure. This could have been a lot worse!"

"Yup, it could have been a lot worse," Dad said.

I asked Mom for a sixth cup of hot chocolate.

"I think you've had enough by now, don't you?"

"Alright," I sighed, with disappointment.

(I sometimes joke my chocolate addiction began that evening!)

"Well, I'm gonna head to bed," said Dad.

"Me too," said Mom.

"Yeah, I'm tired too."

That night, my bed felt extra cottony-soft.

And sleep came easy.

A Lesson

THAT SNOWY SATURDAY is unforgettable. I've endured a multitude of challenges since then, but never have I experienced anything like losing my way in Taylor

1 | LOST IN SOLON

Valley. And while I gleaned many lessons from the situation, one valuable message stands out most.

Some people argue there is no spiritual dimension to life. The British, French, and American Enlightenments of the Seventeenth and Eighteenth Centuries certainly spread such thinking throughout the world, and especially the West.[2]

Skepticism toward spirituality and religion grew. But the American Revolution and four Great Awakenings over the next three centuries saw an increasing shift, once again, toward spirituality and religion.[3]

We now live in an increasingly interconnected world. We interact with people from many places. And we can learn from and appreciate diverse spiritual traditions the world over. Yet, the world is also more complex.

The modern workplace and the impersonal nature of technology,[4] and the increased numbers of disasters and their reporting[5] have left us longing for connection and meaning.

And yet, belying all these changes exists something incredibly unique and unchanging.

The Inner Voice.

We sense a nudge or message from beyond—from a source greater than ourselves.

It penetrates the veil between heaven and earth.

When we hear it, we're suddenly aware we're not alone in the world, but connected, always, to the realm beyond the veil.

Its promptings come in the hustle and bustle of day or in our nighttime dreams.

It's distinct from yet intertwined with our inner world. It's not psychosis or mental illness.

And it is independent of all the religious and sociopolitical changes throughout history.

It's always there. Eternal.

And we can hear it.

If we listen.

~~~

I grew up attending a Presbyterian church. I believed in God. But it wasn't until adulthood that I had a conversion experience, after which I began consciously living my faith and growing spiritually.

Over the years, however, I heard the viewpoint that one cannot hear God prior to conversion. "Beforehand, one is separate from God," they would say. "God doesn't acknowledge sinners!"

But that hasn't been my experience. The same voice I know now was present at age twelve in Solon. As I developed spiritually, however, I learned to heed its direction.

It's a voice unbound by doctrine, space, and time.

Unbound by our own successes and shortcomings.

There at birth and present at death.

Comforting us at our lowest, and with us at our highest.

~~~

I often reflect on that cold Saturday. A profound and pivotal moment. And, as I navigate my journey, I'm aware how easily we can miss God's voice and protection, but how wonderful it is when we listen.

Then, I allowed external persuasion to dissuade me. Ignoring the inner prompting led to serious consequences. I could have died out there in the wilderness at age twelve. I'm grateful that God had other plans!

But the same Voice I ignored, I also eventually acknowledged. I prayed and listened. I chose a direction. An arrow in the snow. Others prayed. Dad and I headed in opposite directions. Our paths crossed. And my life was spared.

When we arrived for the afternoon of skiing, my mother insisted I go ahead. She'd be right there. Her intentions were certainly to help, not harm. Yet, there was The Inner Voice. And I let my mother convince me to avoid its instruction.

That interaction represents a common experience of humankind. Competing voices pull at us from all directions. And yet, therein lies both our challenge and opportunity.

When pondering The Inner Voice—what the Bible calls the *still small voice*[6]—the word *courage* comes to mind. It takes courage to believe our internal, subjective world, where many voices clamor for attention.

Yet, it is courage that connects us—to ourselves, to God, to each other, and to all the wonderful opportunities that endlessly stream toward us.

It also takes openness, willingness, trust, and humility to acknowledge the Divine exists. Doing so requires the dethroning of ourselves as the sole masters of our destiny.

And heeding The Inner Voice is risky. Sometimes we're prompted to step outside our comfort zones to do things that appear foolish to others.

After all, consider Noah! He built a huge ship. While the Bible gives no evidence the people of the day mocked him, such an unusual undertaking could certainly draw scrutiny!

But Noah held firm to the words God spoke to him,[7] while most people were unaware of his project and perished in a world-engulfing flood.[8]

As you read the stories here, I invite you to stir your curiosity—about your life, your inner experience, and the way you navigate your journey.

Are you listening? Perhaps you are a seasoned listener. If so, I invite you to keep listening and growing.

But if you have never considered the spiritual dimension of life or you've lost your way, you can know God. It starts with curiosity. And it looks like this: "God, if you're real, please show me!" Then, open your heart to receive.

When I was lost in Taylor Valley, it took the form of a question and an arrow in the snow. And hours prior, a beckoned, **Go back!**

It was not the last time I heard that voice—the "gut feeling, the hunch, or 'knowing' that defies experience or understanding" (Ellerby 2010, 166).[9] There were many other occasions. Each has been memorable and unique. And I've shared them here to offer you hope, encouragement, and inspiration.

As you read these stories, I invite you to open your heart—to the wonder within and beyond yourself—and listen.

2. UNEXPECTED GRACE

Grace comes into the soul as the morning sun into the world: there is first a dawning; then a mean light; and at last the sun in his excellent brightness.

—Thomas Adams (1583-1652) [1]

EMBARKED ON a new phase of my life in the fall of 1990. College. And to help me prepare, I attended a week-long pre-college summer program at the University at Albany, offered by the New York State Commission for the Blind. The events of that week and the following year—my initial college year at Rensselaer Polytechnic Institute—proved to be profoundly life-changing.

Albany

For one week in August, college-bound visually impaired students from around the state joined on the Uptown campus of the University at Albany to live together in the dorms, socialize, and learn coping and independence skills.

Aaron and I attended together, and we shared a four-room suite in Whitman Hall, located on the State Quadrangle, with two other students.

⁂

The Uptown campus was unique. All gray and white in appearance—limestone, marble, granite, and concrete construction. Everything symmetrical in all directions.

Linear in appearance. Narrow, tall windows. Colonnades and arches. Smooth surfaces and umbrella shell roofing. Open spaces, fountains, pools, and formal landscaping. New Formalism—the mid-twentieth-century institutional and civic architectural style of Edward Durell Stone and Minoru Yamasaki.[2]

A postmodern architectural nightmare for newcomers, the Uptown campus was confusing symmetrical. Losing one's way on campus was typical.[3]

The colonnades, arches, fountains, and covered outdoor walkways made the campus feel more suitable to a southern climate than to Central New York.

But in the summertime, ample greenery accentuated the sprawling gray slabbery. Blooming trees and shrubs filled the planters in the open spaces, altogether casting a sedative aroma over any anxious visitor.

⁂

2 | UNEXPECTED GRACE

Each morning after breakfast, the students and staff gathered in the main lobby of the Campus Center. Red upholstered chairs arranged in a large rectangular pattern spread over the granite floor. Twenty-five students and two instructors.

The rectangular seating arrangement was a new experience for me. In high school the desks were arranged in rows, all students facing forward. There were some exceptions, but that was the norm. And that didn't help me overcome the social anxiety I carried throughout my childhood and adolescence.

But this was different. There were ample opportunities for open dialogue as we sat facing each other. And, as I became aware of my social anxiety in this setting, I acknowledged it as an obstacle to my growth.

I really want to speak up and participate. But I have a lot of anxiety. Do others feel this way?

For the first two days, I wrestled with fear. But the social freedom I saw in some of the students made me jealous, and by the third day, I gained the courage to speak. And it felt good. An important step in breaking the stronghold fear had on me.

How did I get this way? Why me?

These familiar words came to mind as I pondered what life would be like with more freedom.

Years of ridicule and rejection from peers for having albinism and low vision[4] contributed to my guardedness—in addition to my naturally introverted personality.[5]

I knew I'd need to overcome my social anxiety in the coming years to have an enjoyable social life. And I did change, with practice and patience. And God's help.

Evenings presented social opportunities. One evening, as Aaron and I talked together in our suite, Fernando walked in.

"Hey! How you guys doin'?"

"Alright," I said. "How are you?"

"Good, man. Are you guys sure you're good!? I mean, there's been a lot over the past few days!"

"Yeah, I guess so," I said.

"Hey, you guys need to have some fun! A bunch of us are going up to the rooftop! Wanna come?"

"Where?" said Aaron. "What rooftop?"

"The tower!" Fernando pointed toward Eastman Tower at the center of State quad.

Fear gripped me.

"Oh, I don't think that's a good idea. Isn't that off limits?"

"Yeah! But it'll be fun!" he said.

We declined the offer and Fernando left.

I was acutely aware how afraid I was. And while I had realistic reservations about hanging out atop a twenty-two-story building, it occurred to me that I often turned down opportunities because of fear.

Aaron and I found Marc and his black Labrador guide dog, instead. We sat outside on a concrete bench as night fell and talked about many things. The past. The present. The future. Life with blindness and low vision. College. And it was late when we turned in.

⁂

After breakfast, we gathered in the Campus Center, escaping the August heat. Tony, our instructor with a thick New York City accent opened the morning's meeting.

2 | UNEXPECTED GRACE

"Okay, we're gonna move all the chairs. So, everyone, take a chair. Stack it along the side."

"We want to have a lot of room!" said Maria, Tony's assistant, in her bold Puerto Rican cadence. "You're going to get really comfortable!"

This should be interesting.

The commotion faded as each student claimed a seat.

"You can still sit in a chair if it's more comfortable," said Tony. "And there's a carpet there in the center."

I sat on the cool granite floor with my legs crossed.

"Okay. Everybody settled?" said Tony. "Alright. We want to teach you to medicate. It's a very powerful tool that you can use when you're stressed out. Before exams. Or just in general, wherever you are anxious or stressed."

"And, this is not just for college," said Maria. "This is something you can use all of your adult life!"

"Has anyone ever meditated?" said Tony.

Silence.

Then a bunch of noes.

"Okay. No one?" he said. "That's fine. You're going to learn right now."

"And we'll talk about it afterward," said Maria.

I'd never meditated before. Mindfulness practices were still growing in popularity in the United States.[6] And they weren't included in my Christian upbringing.

"Okay. Let's get started," said Tony. "Get into as comfortable a posture as you can. And relax. And when you're ready, go ahead and close your eyes."

"We recommend closing your eyes, but you don't have to," said Maria. "A lot of times it's more effective that way. But not for everyone."

"Now bring your attention to your breath. Just observe your breath. Inhale through your nose. Exhale through your mouth. Even breaths. Relax," said Tony. "As your breathing slows, observe your body relax. And now, bring your attention to the top of your head."

Tony instructed us to relax each part of our bodies from our heads to our feet until we were completely relaxed.

Though I'd never meditated, I was intent on being an immediate master. I relaxed so much I drooled.

Probably *not* necessary!

Thinking back on this, I laugh.

Twenty minutes passed. And it was time to open our eyes.

"Okay. When you're ready, open your eyes. Stand and stretch for a bit," said Tony.

"Let's take a break and we'll come back and talk about what this was like for everyone," said Maria. "Okay? Ten minutes."

Tony approached me.

"You were really relaxed! Really, *really* relaxed!" He chuckled.

I felt my cheeks grow warm.

He saw me drool!

"I definitely was relaxed!"

"And that's good! That's what's supposed to happen," he said. "That's a great start!"

2 | UNEXPECTED GRACE

"Okay, thanks!" I smiled, but inside I cringed.

Too much drool. I could have wiped my mouth with my shirt! How embarrassing.

As Tony walked away, the new friend my brother and I met the previous evening walked up to me. Marc was almost totally blind, but he had a small amount of sight in one eye. From Kingston, he spoke in an obvious New York City accent and he had a sarcastic but playful sense of humor to match.

"So, what did you think of that?" he said with a smirk.

"That was great!" I said. "It was so helpful! I've never experienced anything like it!"

"Really? I couldn't sit still the whole darn time! I was wrestlin' and movin'! I couldn't wait for that whole thing to be over!"

We laughed.

But joking aside, something happened inside me. And I was curious about it.

Facing my social anxiety *and* meditating was a huge blow to my fear and anxiety.

I felt the old walls crack.

※

The following day, during a break, I sat on a bench just off the Campus Center lobby. Marc sat next to me attempting to call a friend on the payphone. Students chatted and the noise level rose.

Suddenly, a strong feeling of gratefulness for life welled up within me.

But then, a feeling of sadness—grief about the many years I internalized fear and pain.

The feeling expanded.

A full-body sensation.
A gut sense I need to be alone.

"Hey Marc! I need to take care of something," I said. "I'll be back."

"Go!" he said with force, as if he knew it was important.

The intensity of his response surprised me, adding to the urgency.

Where can I go that's private?

I scanned the area, but students were everywhere.

The men's room.

I walked in.

"Hello!?"

No response.

I spoke to God with words unfamiliar to me.

God, I'm sorry for the way I've lived. I want you to be in my life.

I cried.

"Jesus, please come into my life! I invite you in!"

What am I saying!?

So spontaneous! And I didn't completely understand it until almost a year later.

Peace! Happiness!

Unexpected Grace.

A new peace and calm settled over me. I felt happy. Brighter. Like when the clouds move and the sun shines.

I was by myself, but not alone.

As I returned to my spot on the bench next to Marc, I knew something special just occurred.

∞

The next morning, I awoke at five thirty.

A gentle breeze drifted in through the open window.

Birds chirped happily in the August sky.
Unexplainable peace!
Wow! Where is the fear?
I gazed out the window at the trees and sky.
The feeling of calm in my soul amazed me. A feeling that everything would be okay, no matter what—forever!
What is this new experience!?
I was excited and intrigued.
The week ended.
Twenty miles away, freshman orientation awaited at Rensselaer Polytechnic Institute. Aaron and I planned to study architecture there. As it turned out, it was a memorable year.

Rensselaer

We arrived at Rensselaer. When Aaron and I emptied the U-Haul, it occurred to me we brought too much stuff. As I carefully placed the rubber tree plant on the pavement and scanned the ground for spots to put everything else, I wondered what college would be like.
Why did we bring plants?
Aaron and I lived in the Quadrangle; myself in White III and Aaron in Hunt I.
Its construction was never complete. The original design, by Alfred T. White, called for a full square, but the builders never finished the third side, leaving it an L-shape instead.[7]
Built between 1915 and 1930, the ivy-covered brick building housed 450 students and was divided into nineteen units.[8] A cozy place to spend freshman year.

After we finished the move, I peeked into a dorm room that had much more in it than mine. I felt assured we hadn't completely overdone it!

Orientation came and went. Classes began. The trees turned red and orange. Warm August breezes gave way to cooler September air. And I adjusted a bit more to this new endeavor called college.

One afternoon when I returned to my dorm room I found a piece of mail stuffed under my door. A survey for new students. I glanced at the orange and white Scantron sheet and figured it wouldn't take long to fill in the twenty bubbles. So, I sat and completed it.

One question stood out. "Do you consider yourself a born-again Christian?"

What's that?

Am I?

I've never heard of that.

Having grown up in a traditional Presbyterian church, the term was unfamiliar. But it seemed important.

Hmm. Maybe I am.

No.

Yes?

Okay, God, if I'm supposed to be a born-again Christian, have me be that by April!

I filled-in the "Yes" bubble and returned the survey to my resident assistant.

2 | UNEXPECTED GRACE

The weeks passed, autumn turned to winter and snow, and college life was busy. Then, something changed. Disheartened with architecture as a major, I felt depressed. I questioned my long-held desires, plans, and purpose.

Between classes, I made trips to the music building to play the piano. It seemed the desire to create music pulled at my heart more than architecture, and this continued into the springtime. A significant development, as I wanted to pursue architecture since sixth grade.

∞

Adding to the sense of upheaval was another piece of mail. This time, however, it wasn't a friendly survey, but a strange letter. I received it in January. And it upset me tremendously.

One afternoon, I made the usual trip across campus to retrieve my mail. Across Fifteenth Street. Up the hill past the Rensselaer Union. Past Cary Hall. And then up the thirty-two wooden steps to The Commons.

Once inside, I approached the long, silver wall of student mailboxes, eyed my box, inserted its key, and pulled out a handful of envelopes.

One from Mom and Dad. Something from the Student Health Center. Athletics. Coupons. And then, something odd with no return address.

On my walk back, I opened the strange envelope. In it was a typed message.

I'll read it when I get back.

I returned to the Quad and White III, ran up the steps, unlocked my door, and flopped on my bed to read the letter.

What is this!?

A full-page message that read like a threat. And at the end was the statement, "If you do not forward this letter to ten people in the next 24 hours, you will die."

The room grew dark. Never had I received such a thing. Immediately, I left with the frightening letter to tell Aaron, his roommate, and their suitemates. They thought it was strange, but they weren't as worried as I.

What was it? A physical threat? A curse? I was young and impressionable. I already questioned my career trajectory. And, spiritually, I was inexperienced, but open. I wondered whether it *was* in fact a curse!

And these were the days when things like this didn't happen. We had no security checkpoints. We didn't worry about terrorism. Or anything close to it.

∞

The letter bothered me so much, I decided to make a phone call. I grabbed the telephone, stretching its cord out the door, around the corner, and into the shared lounge.

Laying on the couch, I called the number I obtained from the college directory for the protestant chaplain. I left a voice message.

Ten minutes later, the phone rang.

I removed the beige 1980s style handset from its cradle and brought it to my ear.

"Hello?"

"Hello. Jason?"

"Yes, this is Jason."

"This is Reverend Bob. I know its late, but I wanted to call you back right away."

"Thank you!"

2 | UNEXPECTED GRACE

"You received some kind of a letter you're worried about?"

"Um. Yeah."

"What year are you, Jason?"

"I'm a freshman."

"How are things going so far?"

"Pretty good. Until this letter."

"I understand. What did this letter say?"

"It's a long letter and at the end it says, 'If you don't forward this letter to ten people in the next 24 hours, you will die.'"

"It sounds like a chain letter. It's probably not anything to worry about. But what does it do to you?"

"What do you mean?"

"Does it turn you on? Make you feel afraid?"

"Makes me afraid. I don't know if it's a real threat or maybe, like, that something spiritual could come from it. Like something bad."

"I understand. Would you like to meet me tomorrow? I can make some time. And we can talk about it more."

Both Aaron and I met Reverend Bob the next day. We had a nice conversation and he prayed with us. My fear vanished and I decided not to read him the full letter. We parted ways and never spoke again.

My worry about the letter faded, but thoughts about the meaning of life stirred in my mind. Curiosity and spiritual longing gnawed at my soul.

In April, Aaron expressed he too felt depressed. It turned out, like me, he questioned whether to continue in architecture school. And, his roommate, a Christian, was a constant influence on him spiritually.

On the evening of April 19, 1990, feeling desperate, he made a phone call. He remembered a Christian radio station that broadcast in the Central New York State area and reached out for help.

The telephone in my dorm room rang. It was Aaron.

"Hello?"

"Hi. Do you remember the Christian radio station in Syracuse?

"Oh, yeah. I remember."

"Well, I called there. I was really thinking about everything and wanted someone to talk to."

"Huh! Okay! Good! What happened?"

"I prayed with this guy, Rick."

"Okay. What about?"

"Well, he explained about salvation. And I prayed to receive Jesus. He's wondering if you'd like to talk to him too."

"Hmm. Okay. Yeah, why not?"

Aaron added Rick to the call.

"Hello, brother!"

"Hello."

"I just spoke to Aaron about some things he's had on his mind. And he told me about you guys. That you grew up in church. But he never really understood the message of the Gospel. So, I shared it with him, and he accepted Christ in his heart. What do you think about that, brother!?"

"Huh! That's interesting."

Rick went on to share the Gospel with me, and when he finished, I also prayed with him.

I didn't make the connection between the events that night and my spiritual experience eight months prior at the pre-

2 | UNEXPECTED GRACE

college program. But when I did, I saw clearly that my spiritual experience then was very personal, and on the phone that night with Rick, my faith became verbal and shared. The April conversation continued what began in my heart a year prior.

Unexpected Grace!

Sometime in the weeks that followed, I recalled the Scantron survey.

I sat back in my chair and swung my feet onto the bed.

God, you sure do have a sense of humor! It's April. You answered that prayer right on time!

It all made sense!

Albany.

The survey, its question, and my prayer.

The threatening letter.

Reverend Bob.

Aaron's desperation.

Rick.

It all pointed in one direction. Toward God!

One evening as I sat at my desk in the architecture studio, a student played music that grabbed my attention.

Go talk to him!

The Inner Voice.

It occurred to me that this voice required a response. The Inner Voice felt more loving than previously. I wanted to obey. To discover where it would lead me. In its presence I felt joy and hope!

I rose from my stool and walked across the bland studio.

"Hey, Erik! So, what are you doing over here?"
"Oh, I'm just finishing up my model. What do you think?"
"Yeah, that's pretty nice. I like it!"
"Thanks! So, what are you up to?"
"I heard your music and thought I'd come over to talk."
"Oh, you like this?"
"Yeah!"
"They're a Christian group."
"Oh, that's nice!"
"Are you Christian?"
"I am!"
"What about your brother?"
"Yes. He is too."
"How long have you guys been Christians?"
"Within the month, officially. Though we grew up attending church."
"That's great! I'm glad to hear that! Anytime you guys want to talk or hang out, let me know."

I heard The Inner Voice more often after that. And I developed a curiosity for responding. And an excitement about this new way of life.

And as May approached, I felt springtime bloom in my heart as much as it did around me. The trees turned green and flowers blossomed. And hope, joy, and peace calmed my heart.

As the school year ended I thought about what to do next. I continually felt pulled to play and create music.

And a new spiritual depth emerged in my life. The Manifest Presence of God.

Fear and Peace

THE WORDS OF the sixteenth-century English preacher, Thomas Adams, beautifully describe grace. "Grace comes into the soul as the morning sun into the world: there is first a dawning, then a mean light, and at last the sun in his excellent brightness" (Adams 1861, 61, par. 2).[9]

During my year in Albany, the sun dawned in my heart. And that was just the beginning. In the years that followed, I found yet a deeper place with God—The Manifest Presence, further emotional healing, life purpose, fellowship with others, and encounters with angels.

But in Albany, God confronted my fears and brought peace—Unexpected Grace. Unexpected, because, though I sought to confront my social anxiety directly, I didn't expect a release from fear, or to hear The Inner Voice more, or to have newfound hope and joy. It all came as a beautiful gift. And so it is for all who seek.

Jesus said, "Ask, and it will be given you. Seek, and you will find. Knock, and it will be opened for you. For everyone who asks receives. He who seeks finds. To him who knocks it will be opened." (Matthew 7:7-8 *Word English Bible* [WEB]).

I stepped toward my fears, and God stepped toward me!

There is a lot we can do to overcome our fears. Meditation, for example, can calm our hearts. The meditative space is timeless, and in a sense, empty—of all the chaos, cares, and calamity of this world. And, therefore, it's also full—of joy, love, and peace. It's the space we go to when we pray.

And, taking steps to do the things we're afraid of teaches us that what scares us isn't scary after all. Developing a sense of wonder about the things we dream of doing, rather than succumbing to fear, can motivate us to action.

But there's a limit to what we can do. Beyond that—beyond ourselves and our own efforts—is grace.

Unexpected Grace!

I've found that reaching toward heaven—even just a little bit—cracks open the door to reveal a beautiful beam of sunlight. Cast across the darkened floorboards of our hearts through a door just ajar, the sunlight of heaven beams in. And as we open the door further, light fills the entire room. A breathtaking experience. Or a gentle calm.

There are many ways God meets us. But regardless of whichever way, just as we welcome the warmth and light of a sunrise, we cherish Unexpected Grace. We move *toward* the light and warmth with a spirit of anticipation and joy.

It would be misleading to say I've never again had heartache. I've journeyed through many trials since my days in Albany.

But what I can say: regardless of what happens in my life, I have joy—"the sun in his excellent brightness" (Adams 1861, 61, par. 2).[10]

3. THE MANIFEST PRESENCE

We are like common clay jars that carry this glorious treasure within, so that the extraordinary overflow of power will be seen as God's, not ours. Though we experience every kind of pressure, we're not crushed. At times we don't know what to do, but quitting is not an option. We are persecuted by others, but God has not forsaken us. We may be knocked down, but not out.

—St. Paul The Apostle [1]

FOLLOWING MY INITIAL college year, I continued opening my heart, and I experienced a tremendous amount of internal healing. I experienced the indwelling

Spirit of God in my heart—The Manifest Presence—for the first time.

It's difficult to pinpoint when and how it occurred, but through steps of faith, therapy that healed years of pain, and worship services where I continually opened my heart—the Spirit entered.

I can only describe my initial sense of The Manifest Presence as a feeling of incredible love and safety; that everything would be okay; that those with whom I worshipped were family.

In such moments, surrounding scenery took on a different appearance—at times like looking through water. And a feeling of *home* accompanied it. Like the best feeling of home and acceptance one could ever experience.

And I knew that as the character of heaven.

That must be what heaven is like!

○○○

This ethereal sense deepened into an internal energy. The Spirit poured into me like water. Like electricity. But not painful by any means. The opposite. And bringing profound internal healing. One must experience this firsthand to truly understand.

Many of my most intense and personal moments with The Manifest Presence occurred in worship services. However, some occurred when I was alone.

○○○

In the spring of 1995, I encouraged Aaron to move to Syracuse. At the time, I attended Syracuse University where I pursued a music degree. He found an apartment on the campus

3 | THE MANIFEST PRESENCE

hill, on Comstock Place. I lived on campus. But I often visited Aaron at his new apartment.

One afternoon, as I lay in the windowsill of the large bay window in his living room, soaking up the mid-March sunshine, I listened to a message by Ravi Zaharias. A tape I'd held onto for a while. And that day I decided to give it a listen. The message was about grace. (You can find the full story in Ravi's book, *Walking from East to West: God in the Shadows*.)[2]

Ravi spoke about Hien Pham, his interpreter in Vietnam. Years after concluding his ministry there, Ravi received a call from Hien explaining he was imprisoned, and that during his sentence, communist propaganda was forced upon him. The deluge was so overwhelming, that on one night, he decided to give up on God. But the next day, during latrine duty, he discovered Bible pages in the trash that someone used for toilet tissue. Hien wept as he read, in English, Romans chapter 8, about God's unfailing love. Then, after his release, he planned an escape from Vietnam, but five Vietcong discovered his plan. They didn't arrest him. They escaped with him!

∞

This incredible message of grace struck me more intensely than any message I'd heard.

And as the recording neared its end, something happened.

That same feeling of gentle pressure and urgency I sensed while sitting in the campus center in 1990 touched my heart.

A tug on my heart. A warmth.
Unexpected Grace.
Find a place to be alone. Now.
The Inner Voice.

"Aaron, do you mind if I lay on your bed for a while to pray? God is really getting my attention!"

"Oh! Sure!" He left the bedroom as I entered.

I laid on his bed just under the window. Outside, the wind howled, winter in full force, all surfaces covered in white.

A powerful energy surged through my soul.

The Manifest Presence!

I don't recall how much time passed as I laid there bathed in waves of the Spirit—the most powerful manifestation of the Spirit I'd experienced.

Internal healing. Relief.

Outside, a sound. A chainsaw? Snowmobile?

Immediately, I was back in Solon, lost in wintry wilderness. I recalled the scariness of losing my way. My rescue. Dad. The ranger. The snowmobile. The warmth of the fire. The healing conversation and hot chocolate.

And then I knew God had a message.

This was like *then*.

In Solon, God rescued me physically. But this day, God rescued me from more than just winter wilderness. He saved me from *me*—from my past wounds and attachment to worry.

Aaron walked in.

"Oh!! I'm sorry!" he whispered. "I just need to get something quick, but I'll go. I really can sense the presence of God!" He laughed softly, then tiptoed out.

When the otherworldly manifestation ended, I rose to my feet, my eyes seeing stars as if I'd seen a bright light.

Outside, the blue-white wintry landscape contrasted with the sunshine I felt inside.

Amazing!

3 | THE MANIFEST PRESENCE

Suffering and Grace

WATER IS ESSENTIAL to life. Humans can function for one-hundred hours without water and for less time in blazing sunlight; a loss of water greater than ten percent of bodyweight, however, is deadly.[3] Many desert animals have unique ways of storing water, allowing them to survive for longer periods without an external water source.[4] But, regardless of their retention capacity, all living beings need water to survive.

Dihydrogen monoxide, however, is but one kind of water.

There is a depth beyond our intellect—beyond our typical psychological experience—where the Spirit of Love fills us. An awakening of soul and spirit. Hidden, yet available to those who seek. And for me, such was the spring of 1995.

Jesus called it living water. He said, "Believe in me so that rivers of living water will burst out from within you, flowing from your innermost being, just like the Scripture says!" (John 7:38 *The Passion Translation* [TPT]).[5]

Imagine that! Rivers of living water flowing from within a person! I've experienced it. Have you!? If not, you can.

The internal experience of the Holy spirit isn't necessarily synonymous with repentance and profession of faith in Jesus. We need to pray for God to fill us. This is the baptism of the Holy Spirit described in Acts. Chapter 2 tells about the disciples' baptism in the Spirit. In chapter 19, Paul shares the baptism of the Holy Spirit with believers in Ephesus.

When the day of Pentecost came, they were all together in one place. Suddenly a sound like the blowing of a violent wind came from heaven and filled the whole house where they were sitting. They saw what seemed to be tongues of fire that separated and came to rest on each of them. All of them were filled with the Holy Spirit and began to speak in other tongues as the Spirit enabled them.

—ACTS 2:1-4 *New International Version* (NIV)[6]

While Apollos was in the city of Corinth, Paul was visiting some places on his way to Ephesus. In Ephesus he found some other followers of the Lord. He asked them, "Did you receive the Holy Spirit when you believed?"

These followers said to him, "We have never even heard of a Holy Spirit!"

Paul asked them, "So what kind of baptism did you have?"

They said, "It was the baptism that John taught."

Paul said, "John told people to be baptized to show they wanted to change their lives. He told people to believe in the one who would come after him, and that one is Jesus."

When these followers heard this, they were baptized in the name of the Lord Jesus. Then Paul laid his hands on them, and the Holy Spirit came on them. They began speaking different languages and prophesying. There were about twelve men in this group.

—ACTS 19:1-7 *Easy-to-Read Version* (ERV)[7]

3 | THE MANIFEST PRESENCE

My association of the two events—my encounter with The Manifest Presence and my rescue in Solon—struck me as an analogy for salvation: for suffering and grace. A comparison of physical to spiritual rescue. Integration and healing. A "making sense" of seemingly senseless suffering.

Perhaps our suffering is not in vain at all, but a part of a larger story or message. The Larger Plan.

Does God speak to us through our suffering? When so often, we think adversity is an antithesis to goodness? In my experience, there *is* a connection.

Peter the Apostle certainly believed so, and it shows in his admonishment of the persecuted churches in Asia Minor. He wrote the following words.

> Beloved, don't be astonished at the fiery trial which has come upon you to test you, as though a strange thing happened to you. But because you are partakers of Christ's sufferings, rejoice, that at the revelation of his glory you also may rejoice with exceeding joy. If you are insulted for the name of Christ, you are blessed; because the Spirit of glory and of God rests on you. On their part he is blasphemed, but on your part he is glorified.
>
> —1 PETER 4:12-14 WEB

God spoke (and speaks) to the world through Christ's suffering—His death and resurrection. So, who are we to believe our suffering has no value or connection to divine suffering and grace? There *is* a connection!

When lost in Solon, cold and tired and at my end, my father found me! And my Heavenly Father found me!

And, Hien Pham, at his very end, when he had no more strength, ready to give up, discovered pieces of Bible pages in the trash which gave him hope, sustaining his faith. And then God provided a way for him and others to escape the country.

The Israelites, lost in the desert for forty years, entered the Promised Land by God's grace!

Our suffering does have meaning!

However, it is difficult to see that meaning while we suffer. Hindsight surely is 20/20. And though I have low vision (about 20/200 acuity), there have been many times I've gained 20/20 clarity—spiritually!

But how many reasons are there for our suffering?

In her book, *When God Weeps*, Joni Eareskson Tada, founder and chief executive officer of Joni and Friends International Disability Center, identified thirty-six purposes of God in our suffering! It's an amazing list! Give it a read.[8]

Indeed, our suffering has a message and meaning. We'll have more peace if we can learn this. But it's a difficult lesson!

The Apostle Paul learned this lesson well. He wrote the following words to the Philippians in response to their support of his ministry.

> For even though you have so little, you still continue to help me at every opportunity. I'm not telling you this because I'm in need, for I have learned to be satisfied in any circumstance. I know what it means to lack, and I know what it means to experience overwhelming abundance. For I'm trained in the secret of overcoming all things, whether in fullness

3 | THE MANIFEST PRESENCE

or in hunger. And I find that the strength of Christ's explosive power infuses me to conquer every difficulty.

—PHILIPPIANS 4:10b-13 TPT[9]

It is also interesting that the story of Hien Pham—about persecution and survival; despair and hope—struck me so intensely. I'd experienced many years of discrimination and rejection prior—especially for having albinism and low vision. But God chose that particular time and message to powerfully communicate that my suffering is not in vain.

And it is also unique to me that this realization came during a powerful and intimate meeting with The Manifest Presence. It seems that such moments often shout the message of suffering and grace with special clarity.

We are but jars of earthen clay. Empty. Breakable. Sometimes kind of plain. Yet, unknown to many, we have a capacity for something otherworldly and extraordinary to move in and through us, if we're open—The Manifest Presence!

Paul the Apostle wrote, "We are like common clay jars that carry this glorious treasure within" (2 Corinthians 4:7 TPT).[10]

Truly, we have much to look forward to as we open our hearts to receive!

4. DESERT AWAKENING

Love is the foundation... Without it religion degenerates into a chattering about Moses and doctrines and theories; a thing that will neither kill nor make alive, that never gave life to a single soul or blessing to a single heart, and never put strength into any hand in the conflict and strife of daily life.

—Alexander Maclaren [1]

SPRING 1999 IS memorable to me. In March I flew from New York City to California to attend a three-month retreat in the high desert, seventy miles north of Los Angeles. At the east end of Los Padres National Forest, three-thousand feet above sea level and nestled on the north face of Libre Mountain, sprawled an old horse ranch—Rancho Corona del Valle. Or, in English, Crown of the Valley Ranch.

The Desert Vineyard Christian Fellowship of Lancaster operated a ministry school on the old ranch, and for three months, I worshipped and learned there with twenty other students from around the world.

It was an exhilarating, life-changing experience that I'll never forget. Not only did I hear God speak to me on multiple occasions; love and grace transformed me.

March

I met Jerry at Los Angeles International Airport at three o'clock in the afternoon. We then hurried to meet three other travelers—one from the United Kingdom and a couple from Australia.

Then, we all piled into a ten-passenger van and made the seventy-mile trip north to Lake Hughes.

Night fell, and the landscape shifted around us. The California highways stretched into narrow roads and introduced the vast, desert landscape.

Joshua trees. Saguaro cacti and barrel cacti. Creosote bushes and pink-flowering prickly pear. Palo verde trees and aloe vera plants. Fan palms and ponytail palms. Century plants and magenta bougainvillea. Fuzzy-looking cholla and red-flowering ocotillo.

All were scattered among the pale desert sand and rocks, as far as the eye could see.

Overlapping mountaintops in the background. Winding roads ahead.

4 | DESERT AWAKENING

We made some small talk. But tired from the long journey, I drifted off to sleep.

∞

The sky was pitch black when we arrived. And as I pulled my bag and fur coat from the back of the van, Jerry appeared.

"Okay! We're here!" he said, standing next to me. "Do you need help carrying anything?"

"No. I think I'm alright."

"That's a really thick coat you have there!"

"Yes, it is!" I smiled.

"I guess you need that back in New York!" he said. "But you won't need it here!"

"Good! I'm looking forward to the warm weather!"

"Okay. You're in Cabin Two. It's the first on the right, up this trail," he said, pointing. "Let us know if you need anything!"

∞

I made my way to Cabin Two. Inside, the walls were cream. The gray carpet appeared freshly vacuumed. A large, arched, California style window covered the wall at one end, and at the opposite end, a loft and bathroom.

I tossed my heavy bag on the floor and curiously looked around. Then I rolled up my winter coat and slid it under the bed where it remained until June.

I heard a knock on the door and opened it. There, stood a short, red-bearded man with silver-framed glasses.

He introduced himself.

"You okay?"

He must notice I'm exhausted.

"I'm okay," I said. "It was a long trip."
"That's fine. I'm Jeff."
I shook his hand. "Nice to meet you, Jeff."
"Make yourself at home!" he said, smiling. "We're getting together in a bit. For some snacks. If you want to join us!"
"Okay. Where?"
"Just down that way, in our dining room," he said, motioning with his arm. "It's the only building that's lit."

I unpacked, and I tested one of the beds for comfort. Three other travelers would soon join me.

I headed down the softly lit trail to the small building housing the kitchen and dining room.

Kathy greeted me as I opened the door.

"Hello! I'm Kathy. Jerry's wife," said the tall brunette. "And you are?"

"I'm Jason."

"Hi Jason! Where are you from?"

"I'm from New York. Syracuse."

"Okay, great! Well, welcome. Grab yourself some food. Something to drink. Sit wherever you'd like."

I knew by the ten o'clock food options, I was in for an enjoyable three months. Pasta. Soup. Cake. Pudding. Soda. Punch. Something else I didn't recognize. It all looked and tasted wonderful.

I carried my plate to one of the indoor picnic tables and introduced myself to some new friends. When finished, I returned to the cabin.

I'm a long way from home. But it'll be a good experience.

I clicked off the light and slid into my soft California bed.

4 | DESERT AWAKENING

※

The following afternoon, I sought some alone time to read and pray. The sunny climate was a welcome respite from the frigid East Coast.

I familiarized myself with some of the trails, and then discovered a patch of tall, dry grass across from the barn and adjacent chicken coop.

That looks like a nice spot.

A moment after making myself comfortable, a tractor on the dirt road behind me interrupted the silence. It's driver, a tall figure dressed in jeans and a blue, plaid shirt waved to me.

※

As the Southern California sun disappeared over the mountain ridge, we shared our second dinner together. I started to feel at home.

And upon exiting the dining room after filling my belly with scrumptious food and my soul with hearty conversation, Kevin, the man from the tractor, greeted me.

"You probably don't remember me, but I saw you earlier when you were laying in the grass by the barn."

"Oh, right! You were on the tractor."

"Yep. That's me!" he said. "I do the grounds keeping and maintenance around here." He twisted an end of his long mustache and smiled. "I tried to get your attention, but then I figured I wouldn't bother you."

"Why is that?"

"Normally, where you were laying isn't a safe spot. There are often rattlesnakes in that area. But they're not out yet. So, I wasn't worried."

"Oh! Thanks for telling me! I'm not used to that back in New York."

"Well, we have them. Just know that's one place to avoid."

Feeling thoroughly welcome, I meandered up the trail to Cabin Two and slept a second night in my soft California bed.

The coming weeks were packed with mornings of worship and speakers. Most were singer-songwriters, for the focus of the three months was worship as a lifestyle. Many of us were musicians.

And after lunch, we worked—some of us on the ground crew and others in the kitchen. I spent many afternoons pulling weeds and rocks, raking branches and leaves, trimming bushes, painting fences, and helping with other landscaping projects.

The cloud of depression that hung over me began to lift. And, as I would later understand, the next three months began my breakaway from a church back home that turned cult-like.

There were many healing opportunities. The words of our speakers, our praise and worship times, and the presence of God saturated our hearts, transforming us from within.

In our worship time one morning, a woman spoke a word.

"I feel God is saying the rattlesnakes are now out, and to be careful."

I glanced upward.

A powerline cast its shadow on the translucent roof window, a snake basking in the sun. The image complimented the woman's words in visual form.

4 | DESERT AWAKENING

God speaks to us in many ways. When we're perceptive, we will hear messages through the *still small voice*,² via our other senses, and from other people. And in some cases, internal or external visions appear in conjunction with spoken words.

The Visual Voice.

In this case, both the shadow and the woman's words crossed in my psyche producing a sense of knowledge.

Yes. The snakes are out.

―∞―

The following afternoon, while casually walking the dirt path to Cabin Two after pulling weeds, I heard a hiss.

A cat!

I love cats, and I knew we had at least one on the ranch. I scanned my surroundings.

"Ssss!"

Huh! I don't see anything. Maybe in the weeds?

I paused, one foot ahead of the other, attempting not to scare the feline.

As I peered into the weeds, I heard it again. Louder.

"Sssssssssss!!"

"Kitty! Kitty! Come 'ere kittycat!" I called out, hoping the furry critter would run my way.

Suddenly, I received a strong internal nudge.

That's not a cat!

The Inner Voice.

I looked around then down at my feet. There, motionless, between my legs, was a long, squiggly snake.

"Sssssssssssssssssss!!!"

I squatted and sprung as high as possible! When I landed, I glanced at the ground behind me. Apparently scared too, the snake slithered away.

Wow! So fast!

Having only caught a quick glimpse of the snake before instinctively jumping, I was unsure whether it was a rattlesnake. It appeared striped. Brown and white.

Were those stripes or diamonds?

I inhaled deeply, calming my racing heart. Later, I mentioned the sighting to Darren, a staff member known for catching, killing, and cooking the rattlesnakes he found.

And the following morning at breakfast, he came to me with the results of his search.

"I found a king snake under Cabin One," he said.

"What do they look like?"

I chose a spot at a table and motioned for him to sit.

"Striped. Brown and white," he said. "This one was."

"You mean like this coffee?"

I peered in my mug eyeing the swirl pattern of coffee and creamer.

"Yeah. Pretty much."

"Are they dangerous?"

"They don't usually bite unless you bother them. And they're not venomous."

"Okay, that's good!"

"So, it probably wasn't a rattlesnake."

"How sure are you?" I forked my pancake and shoved it in my mouth.

"I'm not completely sure. But I haven't yet seen any rattlers in that area this season. Keep an eye out, though. They're out there!" He stood to leave. "Alright buddy, I gotta go. Jerry wants to talk to me."

That was a rattler. I just know it!

No, it wasn't.

Yes, it was!

I got a kick out of my internal battle.

"Come and talk to us," said another student.

I slid my plate over and joined their conversation, already in progress.

─────── ∞ ───────

Some weeks later, on Saturday afternoon, a volleyball game was underway in the sand pit. A circle of staff and students chatted on the lawn. And as I approached them, I heard Kevin and the students talking about a rattlesnake.

"The baby ones are most dangerous," someone said.

I stepped over the stony barrier surrounding the grass.

"Careful Jason!" said Kelly, a student from Australia.

I looked down.

"You almost stepped on a rattlah," she said.

The staff and students broke out in laughter.

"It's dead!" said Kevin.

"I don't see it!"

"Right there on the wall," Kelly said. "It's just a baby!"

"You can pick it up!" said Kevin.

"I'd be careful, Jason! The little bugger might still have venom in 'im!"

I carefully cradled the critter in my hands. It was no bigger than six inches in length and a pencil's width in diameter.

"Fascinating!"

"You'll be fine," said Kevin. "Just don't eat it!"

Eat it!? Why would I?

"Here. Let me see that!" said Kevin.

I handed him the elongated baby reptile.

"So, why are the baby ones so dangerous?" I said.

"The babies can't control their venom," said Ray, a student from California.

"Well, there's actually no proof of that," said Kevin. "But you don't want to get bit by one."

"Hold it up like you're gonna eat it!" I said.

"No, don't do it, mate!" said Kelly.

Kevin opened his mouth and held the snake above his head. As he pretended to eat it, I snapped a photo with my disposable camera. (I still have that picture and laugh when I see it!)

The days grew hotter in the coming weeks. And one afternoon I sought the cool basement of a shared building. Sometimes we gathered there in the evenings to play pool and converse. I imagined no one would be there mid-afternoon. It would be refreshing and quiet.

I rounded the corner of the cabin and proceeded down the stone steps to the basement.

"Oh! Hi Darren!"

"Hey man! Wanna watch?"

"What are you doing!?" I said, noticing long stretches of sliced reptile on sheets of newspaper.

"This is a rattlesnake I found up by my cabin that I caught and killed!"

"Wow! That's huge!"

"Yeah. This is a big one!" he said. "It took me several tries to kill it."

We exchanged a momentary, silent stare. I wondered if he thought the same—that it could have been the snake I saw.

"How'd you do that!?" I said, interrupting the silence.

"I tried to catch it, but I couldn't. I found a large rock and threw it on its head and broke its neck!"

"Wow! Broke. Its neck! Vicious!"

"It took me a several tries."

"That's Cool! So, what are you gonna do with it!?"

"I'm gonna cook it! You wanna try some?"

"Huh!? Um. Try some? Uh. Does it taste like chicken!?"

"It *does* kind of taste like chicken!"

"Great! I think!"

"I don't know if Mary, our chef, will be too happy if I store it in the kitchen freezer though!" he said. "I might have to keep it in my cabin."

"Oh, you have a refrigerator up there?"

"Yeah. But the freezer isn't very big. It'll probably have to go in the kitchen."

"Ha-ha! Maybe she won't notice!"

"Hah! I doubt that. But she'll just have to live with it, won't she?" He smirked.

A week later I tried cooked rattlesnake. It *did* taste like chicken! But tougher.

April

In April, word got around about a certain upcoming event called Summit. A week-long hike. In the desert. With rock climbing. And rappelling.

Late one night, as I conversed in the dining room with Lian from China, Tom from California, and Darren (the snake handler), I noticed some pictures I hadn't seen previously, pinned to the corkboard. People involved in the act of rock climbing and rappelling!

"Huh! Hey, Darren! What are these?"

"What? Oh! That!" he said, grinning. "You had to notice! Well, you'll be doing that soon."

"Doing what?" I turned to look at him.

"I'm actually not supposed to tell you guys yet," he said, lowering his voice. "It's a surprise."

"Surprise!?" said Lian. "What are you keeping from us?"

Darren cracked up.

"You're really getting a kick out of this, aren't you!?" I said.

"Yeah, I am! Anyway, you guys will be hiking through the desert for a week. But, I can't say anything more about it yet."

"Wow! That's rad!" said Tom. "They didn't tell us that!"

I looked at the board more closely.

Those are some tall cliffs!

"Are they trying to keep us from freaking out by putting off telling us?" I said.

More laughter.

"That, and it's supposed to be a surprise," said Tom. "It's really a lot of fun."

As the days passed, other staff confirmed the conversation. I'd like to say I was only excited, but I was also a bit nervous. As were others.

At age twenty-eight I was in decent physical shape. Most of us were. No wonder they screened for height, weight, and physical activity when we applied! But I was concerned whether a journey through the desert might be too strenuous for some of us.

4 | DESERT AWAKENING

And I imagined how easily one could get lost in the desert. And how horrific that would be. I was lost once in the winter, and I didn't need a summer version to compliment it.

<hr />

The Israelites of yore, in their exodus from Egypt to the Promised Land, wandered forty years in the desert wilderness of the Sinai Peninsula—a trip that otherwise would have taken them eleven days![3]

Our trip would span seven miles over the course of a week, hopefully without issue. And its purpose? To experience desert life as the Israelites had—and have fun doing it!

<hr />

Shortly after breakfast one morning in April, we jammed into two large vans and headed to Joshua Tree National Park, where the Mojave and Sonoran deserts met.

Three and a half hours later, we arrived.

Before us spanned a massive landscape of sand, mountains, blue sky, and no civilization!

I stepped out of the van onto the hot earth, feeling small amidst the vast wilderness.

What do we do now?

"Okay, make sure you have everything you need," said Jerry. "We're meeting right over there in a few minutes!" He pointed to an unencumbered sandy space across the road.

A buzz of commotion stirred as the students and staff gathered their gear and belongings.

"Take a backpack from the pile," said Mike, one of our guides for the journey.

"We're going sit in a circle," said Al, our other guide. "Just relax. Take some time to wind down from your trip, and we'll get started in a few minutes."

Mike and Al taught us about desert safety, including hydration, reptiles, and first aid. And sooner than expected, we walked away from our safe sand circle into the beautiful but forbidding desert sandscape.

There is a unique way one must walk in the California desert. A kind of meandering—around cacti, Joshua trees, and rocks. Rarely a straight path. And with heavy packs on our backs, the motion shifted our weight around. A similar feeling to skiing moguls.

Left. Right. Left. Right.

And constantly monitoring one's footsteps while not losing sight of the group is crucial. Tripping hazards abound. And this too required a continual motion. Looking up and ahead. Then down at one's feet.

Up. Down. Up. Down.

With time, the rhythm felt therapeutic. A kind of secret desert language only known to the desert and her voyagers.

Left. Right. Left. Right.

Up. Down. Up. Down.

Water must be in reach. Either held in the hand or stored in one's pack. With at least one hand free for grasping, clutching, and climbing.

Then there's the exhaustion. One must monitor energy reserves and respond to the need for rest. But it's personal. Everyone needs a break at different times. One must learn to take short breaks without losing sight of the group and be willing to answer frequent inquiries from others, such as "How are you doing?"

―――― ∞ ――――

By evening, we reached out first campsite. Though tired from the afternoon hike and sweltering desert heat, we set up our four-person dome tents. We made dinner together as dusk fell. And after dinner, we sat around a fire, talked, sang, and prayed. And we repeated this pattern for a week: hike, set up camp, cook, campfire, sleep, breakfast. Repeat.

Making dinner in the desert offered an unspoken message of cooperation and humility. We operated a rotating cooking and cleanup crew. The importance of cleanliness and safety couldn't be overemphasized.

And the most surprising aspect of desert meals was they were amazing! Maybe it was that we were famished by dinnertime. Or maybe the food was actually yummy!

―――― ∞ ――――

One of the most memorable times was the night we slept without tents.

"The weather is good," said Mike. "There won't be any rain tonight."

"It's just something you must do if you're going to roam the desert," said Al. "There's nothing like it!"

"What about the bloody snakes, Mike?" said Logan from Basingstoke, England.

"Rattlesnakes are not really aggressive. They tend to avoid humans. Usually problems only arise when people bother them."

"Well, alright! That's quite relieving! I'd be gobsmacked to find one in the middle of the night!"

The day's heat dissipated into a comfortable seventy degrees, the sky clear and midnight blue.

We rolled out our sleeping bags under the stars.

I chose a spot next to a teddy bear cholla cactus. And on my opposite side a creosote bush functioned as a curtain between me and the others.

"Hey dude, are you sleeping in your clothes?" said Kyle over the bush.

"Just a tee shirt and underwear, I think."

"Really? I think I'm gonna sleep in my clothes."

"Okay. Well, I'm gonna keep a pair of jeans next to me in case it gets cold."

"Sounds good, man."

I fluffed my pillow (yes, we brought pillows), made myself comfortable, and zipped up my sleeping bag. Then, I laid on my back, gazing into the perfect night sky, in awe at the sight.

An arm of Milky Way Galaxy stretched across the vast night canvas. Stars speckled and filled in the background. The moon, a perfect crescent off to one side. The air, fresh and crisp. The Creator's limitless painting.

And somewhere during my nighttime thoughts, prayers, and amazement, I drifted off to sleep.

Desert awakening came in an instant. I slept straight through the night and awoke completely refreshed. The sun peeked over the horizon and the sky shone a pale blue. I breathed in deeply and exhaled the fresh morning air.

That was the best night of sleep I've ever had!

4 | DESERT AWAKENING

Laying in my sleeping bag, I imagined we were meant to sleep on the ground and that somehow the world was deceived into using beds, an apparently less-comfortable option, and that I'd never need a bed again.

∞

Our trip was free of rain—until our final campsite. But, at the time, Mike, Al, and our staff declined to tell us it was our final site, wanting to keep us in the desert mindset.

As we hiked to the campsite, I felt something cool and moist on my arms and neck.

Rain!? Yes! That's rain!

"Okay, set up your tents as quickly as you can," said Jerry.

The sparse raindrops increased in frequency.

As our four-man crew set up our tent, rainwater collected at its base.

"Uh-oh! We gotta do something about this!" I said. "There's water collecting!"

"Okay! I've got a solution!" said Caleb.

Using a branch, Caleb dug a trench around the tent and connected it to a makeshift drainage pool.

During the night, frequent thunderclaps exploded in the desert silence. Flashes of blue-white lightening illuminated the solid darkness. And the sound of unrelenting rain, like gunshots, pelted our waterproof tents.

I awoke, my right foot cold and wet.

What's happening!? Is the tent leaking!?

I sat up to investigate the situation, realizing I shifted in my sleep. A bottom corner of my sleeping bag lay in the water-filled trench.

Oh, no! The trench isn't draining!

Too tired to fix the problem, I removed my socks, curled up, away from the problem, and fell back asleep.

The following morning, I awoke unrested. My only rough desert awakening of the trip.

"Uh! That was a rough night!" I said to the other tent dwellers.

"Really!?" said Will. "I slept fine. What happened?"

"The end of my sleeping bag fell in the trench!"

"Oh Jay! Why didn't you get up and fix it?"

"I guess I could have. But I was too tired."

"You should put your sleeping bag in the sun today."

"Yeah, that's a good idea. If it doesn't storm again."

"Let's pray that doesn't happen!" Will said.

"Okay, I'm getting out of this tent now! I'm hungry!" I unzipped the front flap, revealing a sunny sky and crisp, post-storm air.

A good breakfast, which remedied my mood, was especially important. As it turned out we needed plenty of energy.

"Today we're rock climbing and rappelling!" said Al, as we gathered around for breakfast. A mass of climbing gear displayed itself on a nearby picnic table, inviting curiosity.

After breakfast, Mike and Al packed up the gear. Then, we climbed into the rocky mountainside to pray in silence before our ascent to the jumping-off place.

Once we reached the mountaintop and secured our harnesses, we attached our carabiners to a shared safety line and made our way to a precarious ledge.

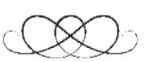

4 | DESERT AWAKENING

Leaning back into the harness as Mike and others manned the ropes, fear rose from my gut to my throat.

Will this hold?

I righted myself.

"Is everything's secure!?"

"Nah, we're just going to let you plunge to your death!" said Mike.

"Really funny, mate!" said Timmy, Kelly's husband.

"Yeah! Really funny!" I said.

Composing himself, Mike double-checked my harness and the ropes. "Yeah, you're good."

Again, I leaned back, this time trusting the equipment with my full weight.

That's relieving! It works!

A combination of courage and fear surged within me.

"Your right rope is the most important! That's your brake!" said Mike. "Pull it to stop and loosen it to lower yourself. But *do not* let go of it!"

After climbing past the rocky budge at the top of the one-hundred-foot cliff, I paused, turning to the horizon behind me. Exhilaration surged through my soul as I gazed upon the marbled sky and endless desert.

And when my feet met the ground, a feeling of accomplishment welled up inside me. I then joined the students who finished rappelling and sat on a rock next to them. We cheered on the remaining mountaineers.

For most of us, it was our first-ever rappel. And we each had unique reactions to the endeavor. For Will, a staff member accustomed to rappelling with the students, it wasn't a big deal. Others expressed excitement as I had. Timmy, however, wouldn't trust the harness. We encouraged him from the base of the cliff, but it was too much for him. He cried audibly, and finally declined the venture altogether.

I felt disappointed for Timmy. I wanted him to know the thrill. But no stranger to fear, I felt tremendous compassion for him. Something in his past—or present—gripped him, robbing him from the wonder of the moment.

And that's what fear does—until we face it, head-on, and overcome its suffocating hold.

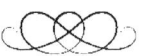

When we returned to the campsite, three ropes hung from the rockface.

"After lunch, we're going to climb," said Mike. "It is optional. We know you might be tired at this point, so it's better to be safe than try to climb if you're too tired. But we'd like to encourage you to. If you can. So, eat a good lunch and we'll get started afterward."

I picked the one-hundred-foot rope and climbed eighty-five percent of the way to the top as Lian belayed. Then, I manned the ropes as she climbed.

Climbing and rappelling was an existential experience. We stared fear in the face as we risked potential injury and death. And for me, on the other side of fear, I found untold joy. Each of us gleaned important life lessons.

As we chatted around the fire that evening, Mike and Al invited us to ask questions about their wilderness experiences.

From the other side of the firepit, a student spoke.

4 | DESERT AWAKENING

"What are you guys thinking when you're holding the ropes for us!?"

Silence.

Then Mike yelled out, "Will! This! Hold!?"

The entire group erupted in laughter.

―✿―

The next morning, we packed up camp as usual and proceeded to our next site. But soon we saw vehicles. Our vans. Our week-long journey concluded. I felt sad, but also relieved!

First, however, a trip to Pizza Hut! Jerry spoke with the restaurant manager before we entered, for our group was large, and we were quite soiled from a week without showering! He welcomed our business and we consumed an inordinate amount of pizza. Then, we made the three-hour journey back to Lake Hughes.

I immediately headed to Cabin Two upon our arrival. And as I relaxed under my first shower in a whole week, I thought about the events of the past seven days—a beautiful, challenging, unforgettable experience!

May

In May, some in our group fell ill. A couple of weeks later, I too felt nauseous. And it wasn't from eating rattlesnake!

One night, as I sat alone in the classroom building, playing the piano and creating songs, I grew concerned about the sickness going around.

I thought of Jesus's words:, "Ask, and it will be given you. Seek, and you will find. Knock, and it will be opened for you."[4]

I prayed.

Why are we getting sick, God? Show me the solution.
I closed my eyes.
I waited.
A bottle of water.
The Visual Voice of God produced an image of a water container in my mind, and it occurred to me there was a problem with the drinking water.

I recalled Mary stocked bottled water in the pantry next to the classroom.

The pantry was full of boxed and canned goods, snacks, and water. Mary kept the pantry unlocked so we could grab snacks at will.

I went in and ripped open a pack of Poland Spring, grabbed one, and set out for a late-night walk. As I drank the water, my stomach calmed.

In the morning, I felt completely recovered. I mentioned the concern to Jeff, and going forward, we boiled our dishwater.

Some chose to drink the bottled water as I did. But those who continued to drink tap water remained ill.

Shortly after the retreat concluded in June, I got word the town tested the water and it was positive for fecal matter.

Subsequently, the staff examined the plumbing and discovered a break in a sewer line. Sewer water leached into the drinking water, making us sick.

The discovery confirmed my vision. Fresh water was the answer. And the only source of fresh water was the stock of bottled water in the pantry.

I received the vision because I *asked*. Remember Jesus's words. "Ask, and it will be given you. Seek, and you will find. Knock, and it will be opened for you" (Matthew 7:7 WEB).

More Than Words

THREE MAIN THEMES emerged from my desert awakening: *messages and manifestations, faith and courage,* and *love and community*. Each theme highlights an important aspect of spiritual awareness and development. Together, they underscore that faith, when well-lived, is both personal and communal.

Messages and Manifestations

Warnings about snakes and contaminated water were far from the only messages I received during the three months. And, while the Divine protects us, other kinds of messages can come our way. Messages may provide direction, give hope for the present or future, or offer correction.

And when we are truly perceptive, we will also receive messages from various sources, such as through our circumstances, nature, music, our nighttime dreams, and the Bible.

Divine communication often is more than words. This is especially true of the Spirit and the experience of grace.

In the stories you've read so far, providential communications have come to me through The Inner Voice, Unexpected Grace, The Manifest Presence, The Visual Voice, and the words of other people. You'll read more about The External Voice in chapter 7. And in chapter 8, you'll read about The Divine Cinematographer and The Divine Script.

Faith and Courage

Fear and courage were prominent themes during my three-month journey. And they are crucial components of personal development and divine involvement in our lives.

My experience of leaning into and trusting the harness while rappelling is much like opening our hearts to God. Like rappelling, faith requires a transfer of weight—from reliance on our own strength to reliance on the Almighty.

And the transformation of fear into exhilaration once I surpassed the cliff's edge is like overcoming our fears in daily life. When we face and conquer our fears, they crumble, revealing beautiful vistas we've never seen.

But trusting the Divine is a process. Each step to dismantle the grip of fear—regardless of the step's size—is insurmountably valuable.

We must not be disappointed if this takes time.

We'll make mistakes along the way. Sometimes we'll choose fear over faith. Sometimes we'll falter or fail. However, most important, is to take another step. To lean in again. And to never give up.

And while the message to *be not afraid* permeates the Bible, and peace is a sure fruit of a life lived in tune with the Spirit,[5] fear is not an element we should eradicate completely from our lives. Fear is hardwired in our biology and is helpful for many functions, such as signaling danger.[6]

We'll never get rid of all fear, nor should we. But we can learn to overcome the kind of fear that robs us from joy, hope, purpose, and a relationship with God.

If we let fear rule us, all we could be—our goals, dreams, purpose, and calling—goes unlived.

Dr. Roxanne van Voorst, an expert on fear management and courage-building, explained, "Counter to every fear runs a desire. In other words: if you don't do things because you are scared of doing them, it means a part of who you are, remains hidden. Your fear overshadows that part of you" (Van Voorst 2020).[7]

When we face our fears, however, we dispel the shadows and emerge into the hopeful light of our purpose and potential.

The degree and expediency to which we trade the tight grip of fear for peace, however, depends only partly on our acts of courage and faith. The other influence is *love*.

There is a reciprocal nature to spiritual growth that goes like this. The more we exercise faith and courage, the more we receive love and grace, and live in peace—regardless of the circumstances around us. And conversely, the more we allow divine love and grace to fill and changed us, the less we fear and the more we trust. We can start from either point.

Regarding *faith and courage* leading to *love and grace*, the Gospel according to Mark tells the following story.

A woman who suffered for years with a bleeding disorder, though she spent all her money on doctors who couldn't help her, believed Jesus would heal her if she touched him. In a large crowd, she reached out and touched his clothes, and was immediately healed. Jesus said to her, "Daughter, your faith has made you well. Go in peace, and be cured of your disease" (Mark 5:34).

Regarding the power of *love and grace* to dispel *fear*, John the Evangelist wrote to the gentile believers in Ephesus around AD 100,[8] "There is no fear in love. But perfect love drives out fear, because fear has to do with punishment. The one who fears is not made perfect in love" (1 John 4:18 NIV).[9]

Sometimes leaning into the harness is exactly what is needed. At other times, when the jump is too scary, we need mercy and grace. Sometimes it's about giving; other times it's about receiving.

Faith and love are the tools that wrench us from fear, self-doubt, complacency, sadness, and depression, and into the realm of amazing vistas.

When we live in this realm beyond words—the realm of faith, courage, and love—we come alive!

Love and Community

My time in California was truly an awakening—imbued with the Spirit and love. I felt like I emerged from a deep sleep.

And we experienced *no* interpersonal problems during the three months. I recall the program director remarking one evening as we met together in the shared lounge, that he never witnessed such an example of love in Christian community. He teared up as he said, "You did it!" It was truly a special moment I'll never forget.

Within all providential communication—whether for protection, direction, hope, healing, reassurance, correction,

4 | DESERT AWAKENING

or something else—is the loving personality of the Divine. By this, we know we hear God's—and not another's—voice.

And when individuals who truly know God's love unite, they create loving communities. Conversely, when individuals join, but operate without love, they create unloving communities. It can take but one or a few people to enhance or destroy the energy of a place.[10]

When we're perceptive, we'll notice the energy of our communities—families, homes, neighborhoods, churches, schools, organizations, states, nations, the world. And through awareness we can implement change.[11]

Ultimately, however, communities can only improve when they acknowledge their situation and make change a reality. In some cases, outside help is needed. And in the most difficult cases, new leadership might be best.

In California, however, it felt as though we breathed love! What an experience!

Two stories, one from the Bible and another from fourteenth-century literature illustrate well, that love is the greatest virtue in our lives and communities.

The first story is from the Bible.

The Corinthian church, around AD 53-55, divided over theology and various customs, lost sight of holiness and genuine love; they argued about who among them was greatest based on their spiritual gifts.[12]

In his letter to the Corinthians, Paul the Apostle countered that their gifts would pass, but that faith, hope, and love will last forever.

> Love never fails. But where there are prophecies, they will be done away with. Where there are various languages, they will cease. Where there is knowledge, it will be done away with. For we know in part and we prophesy in part; but when that which is complete has come, then that which is partial will be done away with . . . For now we see in a mirror, dimly, but then face to face. Now I know in part, but then I will know fully, even as I was also fully known. But now faith, hope, and love remain—these three. The greatest of these is love.
>
> —1 CORINTHIANS 13:8-10, 12-13 WEB

The greatest virtue is love. And interestingly, of *faith*, *hope*, and *love*, the word *love* appears the most in the Bible.

Through a survey of sixty English versions of the Christian Bible, I found that—on average—the word *hope* occurred 162 times, *faith* occurred 417 times, and *love* occurred 567 times.

Love is comprised of more than words. And even so, love is a language—sometimes verbal but often nonverbal. And we should yearn to know and express all its forms, whether *xenia* (guest-love or hospitality), *philia* (friendship love), *storgē* (familial love), *éros* (romantic love), *philautia* (self-love), or *agápe* (the love between God and mankind).[13]

Love is from God. John the Evangelist wrote, "Beloved, let's love one another, for love is of God; and everyone who loves has been born of God, and knows God" (1 John 4:7).

The second story I've chosen to highlight the importance of genuine love in community is Geoffrey Chaucer's *The Canterbury Tales*.[14]

4 | DESERT AWAKENING

A group sets out on a pilgrimage from London to Canterbury to receive the blessing of Thomas Becket, Archbishop of Canterbury.[15]

Before their journey, they meet at the Tabard Inn where the host, Harry Bailey, challenges them to a storytelling contest. They each tell two stories on the way to and from Canterbury to pass time; the winner receives a free meal from the inn, paid for by the other pilgrims.[16]

Chaucer's pilgrims came from every class. An element he used for social satire of each character.[17] Madame Eglantine, the Prioress, was no exception.

She wore a bracelet with the inscription *amor vincit omnia*.[18] In English this means *love conquers all*.[19] She, however, was enigmatic and contradictory, her true nature cloaked in false piety—a supposed devotee to Christ but concerned more with her appearance and worldly affairs; an aristocrat turned nun.[20]

༺✥༻

Both the Prioress and the Corinthians had a thing in common. They were concerned with their external appearance but lacked genuine, heart-based love and truth. But pure love is not a façade, not just an outward appearance of righteousness.

When we fully open our hearts to the Divine, *amor vincit omnia*, inscribed on our hearts, overflows from within—*without* pretense. The result is a communal spirit of peace that subdues pride, self-importance, arrogance, hatefulness, and pettiness.[21]

༺✥༻

Our communities are a gift. Unfortunately, we too often take them for granted. And this is true on every level—the world, nations, states, local communities, schools, churches, organizations, and our homes.

We must cherish our communities and protect them with shared love and compassion, for communal freedom can disappear in an instant.

Freedom in the World, an annual report published by Freedom House that tracks worldwide trends in civil liberties and political rights, showed in 2017,[22] only forty-five percent of the world's nations were free. Thirty percent were partly free. And twenty-five percent had no freedom.

Further, the report showed dramatic declines in freedom throughout the world. And, while Burkina Faso, Somalia, and the Central African Republic saw some gains in freedom, only one country in the world made significant strides: Colombia.

In 2018,[23] the report showed continuing declines in freedom throughout the world, but improvements were seen in Uganda, Timor-Leste, Ecuador, and Nepal.

And in 2020,[24] the report showed many countries, including Canada, experienced moderate declines in freedom, while sixteen nations saw significant losses—especially Benin and the Pakistani-occupied part of Kashmir. But some nations experienced modest improvements, and eight saw marked improvements—especially Sudan, Ethiopia, and Madagascar. Many countries, such as the United States, saw no change.

The 2020 report also showed that half of the world's democracies declined in freedom over the past fourteen years and that the United States fell below its traditional democratic peers in the past decade.

Dietrich Bonhoeffer wrote eloquently about community and freedom in *Life Together* ([1954] 2009).[25]

He spoke of Christian fellowship as a gift of grace, invaluable to lonely individuals but taken for granted by those who enjoy it without restriction. He warned we must thank God for this gift, as it can be taken from us.[26]

Summary: More Than Words

In summary, we must love to the degree that *amor vincit omnia* shines in our communities and the world.

The epigraph for this chapter—from nineteenth-century British preacher Alexander Maclaren—expresses this well.

> Love is the foundation of all obedience. Without it morality degenerates into mere casuistry. Love is the foundation of all knowledge. Without it religion degenerates into a chattering about Moses and doctrines and theories; a thing that will neither kill nor make alive, that never gave life to a single soul or blessing to a single heart, and never put strength into any hand in the conflict and strife of daily life.[27]

A love that's personal yet shared; celebrates life but conquers hatred and iniquity; subdues all threats to freedom.

The foundation. The *sine qua non*. The one thing without which we have nothing at all.

Much more than words!

5. A NEW HOME

Nature uses only the longest threads to weave her patterns, so that each small piece of her fabric reveals the organization of the entire tapestry.

—Richard Feyman [1]

MY DESERT JOURNEY came to an end early one sunny, California morning in June of 1999. Will drove me to Las Angeles International Airport to catch my flight back to New York. And I underestimated the time we needed for travel. We shouldn't have stopped at McDonald's. We arrived at Terminal Two just before my flight's scheduled departure.

As I rushed though the Security, someone stopped me.
"Sir!"
I snapped my head around. A security officer.
"What is this!?"
"Oh. That's a box cutter. I use it for work."
"You can't take this on the plane, sir!"
"Sorry about that."
"Well, if you need it sir, you can take it!"
"No. That's alright. I can get another one."
"Are you sure!?"
"Yeah. It's alright."
Crap! That didn't look good.
"I'm definitely not going to make it, Will!"
"Oh, Jay! Okay, let's go sit down and figure out what we're gonna do."

We sat on a bench along the windows overlooking the traffic on World Way.

"I'm going to try to get you another flight."
"That would be really nice of you."
"I have to. My boss is gonna be so upset with me when he finds out!"
"Really? Jerry will be upset?"
"Yeah. He will be really upset. Because I inconvenienced you. We shouldn't have stopped for coffee."
"Well, it's my fault we didn't get going earlier."
"I have a way with this kind of thing," said Will. "You need something better than American Trans Air anyway. I'm going to see if I can get you on a United Airlines flight."
"Okay. Well, I would really appreciate that."

5 | A NEW HOME

Will walked to terminal six to present my case at United. And as I waited, I realized I wouldn't make it on time to meet my pastor, Simon, who was on his way to New York City to pick me up.

I headed to a pay phone to call another church member.

"I'm not going to make it to New York in time," I said into the phone. "Can you call Simon? I don't have his number."

"You're not? Okay, I'll let him know right away!"

I returned to the bench and waited.

Oh, here he comes. Finally!

"I got you on a United flight at no extra cost!"

"That's great, Will!"

"You need to come with me to finalize it. Follow me!"

An hour later, I boarded the United Airlines flight only to learn it would not depart due to a mechanical problem.

Now I'm nervous!

After a six-hour wait in the terminal, finally, a new plane arrived in the empty space next to the ramp.

I found my seat and sank into it, exhausted. I looked forward to seeing my family and friends.

I arrived at John F. Kennedy Airport at two-thirty in the morning, more exhausted than previously. I hitched a cab to the Greyhound station in Manhattan, bought a ticket, and waited until five in the morning for a bus home.

As I rested my sleep-deprived body against a support column in the station's basement, I reflected on the past three amazing months, determined not to let the rocky trip home steal away my joy.

Finally, the bus arrived for the four-hour trip to Syracuse.

Halfway through the trip, the driver spoke.

"Does anyone know where to go from here?"

Unbelievable!

I shook my head.

Another passenger rose and walked to the front to instruct the driver.

Why did I do this just to save money?

I could have flown between Syracuse and Los Angeles for twice the cost, but instead, I chose a cheaper option. A roundtrip flight out of New York City.

Determined to never make such a mistake again, I leaned my head against the window and slept.

I opened the door to the house I shared with three other guys. A mound of dishes stared at me from the kitchen. No one was home. The atmosphere felt heavy. I wanted to leave.

A Mysterious Caller

Things weren't right at church. Most denied it, including the pastor. But I felt it. I knew something was wrong. And I had plenty of evidence. I was ready to leave. Then I received a message from a mysterious caller. Everything would soon change.

The pastor slept with women in the church. He was involved in violent acts with some of the guys. And there were

5 | A NEW HOME

drugs and alcohol. And my friend John, who recently left the church confirmed my suspicions.

The once-vibrant church where I experienced healing and change degraded into a cult. Most of the problems were hidden. But the atmosphere felt heavy.

My California journey healed and awakened me. And when I returned to Syracuse, I knew what I needed to do. I quit the internship I started with the pastor nine months prior and stopped attending most of the meetings.

One of the guys I lived with, Adam, gave me a hard time.

"You need to shit or get off the pot!" he said, one afternoon. He meant that I needed to commit to something or leave the church.

Sickened by this atmosphere, I questioned why I stayed for so long.

In December, Aaron and I made our usual trip to Cortland to visit our parents for the holidays. And after the holidays, I returned to my job as a grocery stock clerk.

On one afternoon in early January, as I checked the employee schedule posted at the service desk, Marcia, the church worship leader walked in.

"Where were you!?" she scolded. "And your brother!?"

"We went to Cortland to visit our family. Like we always do at this time of year."

"Well, you could've let me know you'd be out of town!"

"I could have. But I didn't think it would be a big deal. Especially at Christmas."

"Well, Simon says he's never seen a family so close!"

I was shocked that Marcia appeared at my workplace and verbally accosted me, and at Simon's statement.

Don't you dare interfere with my family!
This has turned into a cult!

I turned and walked away.

A few days later I stepped down from the worship team where I played saxophone.

Dale, another church member, visited the house where I lived with three guys from the group.

"Hey, man! You're back!"

"Indeed!"

"I keep getting calls from this guy who is looking for you and Aaron."

"Really? Who is it?"

"I can't remember his name. He says he knows you guys."

"Huh. I can't think who that might be."

"I'm not sure if I still have the message. But, when I get home, I'll look, and if I have it I'll give you a call."

That evening, the phone rang. It was Dale.

"The guy's name is Rick."

"Oh! I know who it is!"

"Who is it?"

"He's the guy who shared Christ with Aaron and I about ten years ago."

"Do you still have the number?"

"Um. Hold on."

"Yeah, that would be great if you still have it"

"Okay, you ready?"

"Yeah. Go ahead."

5 | A NEW HOME

It was a Syracuse number, so I figured Rick must not live too far away.

Rick answered the phone.

"Ten years, brother! It's great to hear your voice!"

"Thanks! I'm so glad to get in touch with you. It's been a long time!"

"So, how did you get Dale's phone number?"

"Oh, is he the guy I left the message with?"

"Yeah."

"Well, that's the number Aaron gave me when I ran into him at March for Jesus last summer."

"Oh, right! He did tell me he saw you. That number would have been Aaron's, but Dale took it with him. Aaron moved into the apartment where Dale and two other guys from the church lived."

"He took Dale's place."

"Right."

"Okay. That makes sense. I was wondering, 'Who is this guy!? And why won't he pass on my message to you guys!?'"

"Oh, yeah. I know. That's kind of how things are here. I'm sorry about that. I think Dale was just trying to protect us from something weird. He didn't know who you were. To him you were just a mysterious caller."

"I know. But I did say I knew you guys."

"Right."

"Well, how are you doing, brother?"

"Things are a bit rough here. Things aren't going well with church. Aaron and I are thinking about leaving."

"I'd like to have you and your brother over. We'll talk and catch up. I'll make you guys a nice dinner!"

"That sounds wonderful! Where do you live now, and when do you want to get together?"

"I'm in Solvay. Where are you?"

"The University area."

"Oh! It's just a twenty-minute drive. What are you guys doing Friday night?"

"Nothing."

"Well, give me your address, and I'll come and get you Friday at dinner time. And we can swing over and get your brother too."

"That's great! I'm looking forward to it—after ten years!"

"Ten years."

"Okay, see you Friday. What. About six?"

"Six o'clock sounds good, brother!"

"Okay. See you then!"

Friday came. Rick arrived in his red pickup. I remembered him as a big guy with long hair. Now he was slim with a short haircut.

We picked up Aaron. The three of us, crammed in the front seat, headed to Solvay for dinner and conversation. And we met together once a week for the next two years. Our meetings helped me transition to my next life phase.

An Unexpected Message

I walked to John and Juliet's apartment. They both left the church while I was in California. And Simon and his inner circle talked poorly of them because of it. But John and Juliet were good friends, always kind and caring to Aaron and me.

5 | A NEW HOME

Later that evening I received an unexpected message—from God!

I sat and talked for hours with John and Juliet. Their small apartment was decorated with strings of Christmas lights they kept up yearlong. Tie dye tapestries covered the windows.

We talked until we were tired. Then John offered to drive me home.

"I'll give you a ride," said John.

"Alright. But can you drop me off a block early? Like at the intersection of Miles and Broad?"

"Why?"

"Because. The guys are giving me a hard time about everything. And they hate you for leaving. I don't want any more conflict."

"Alright. I can do that."

"Okay. Thanks!"

I hopped in the passenger's side of John's 1985 Toyota van. We talked as he drove.

"Yeah, you really should consider leaving, Jason."

"I know. I want to. I just need to figure out how. I've been looking for an apartment. There's this one in Solvay I like. I have an appointment to see it Saturday."

"Good. Okay. So, I guess I'm dropping you off here."

"Yup. Thank you!"

John smiled, then gave me a hug. "I love you."

"I love you too. Thanks for being a good friend."

I exited his van into the darkness.

Standing at the intersection of Broad Street, Fellows Avenue, and Miles Avenue, I glanced at the house directly in front of me. Across the street, in the shadowy night, sat a duplex house I'd not noticed before.

You're going to live there someday!

The Inner Voice.

The message surprised me. It was clear. I was sure it wasn't just my thoughts.

Huh! Interesting. Well, God, if that's true, let it be so. But, for now, I give this back to you.

Time passed and I forgot about the occurrence.

Solvay

Saturday came. Rick and I headed to Solvay to check out the apartment.

Solvay has a unique history. James Geddes, an engineer, surveyor, New York State legislator, and United States Congressman—who, along with engineer Benjamin Wright, planned the Erie Canal—founded the village in 1794.[2]

Solvay is also home to Crucible Industries, a steel plant in operation since 1876.[3] The factory casts a continuous hum over the village that's increasingly audible the closer one travels toward State Fair Boulevard.

"I like it. I'll take it," I said to the agent.

"Okay. Sign here."

Situated at the south end of Charles Avenue, the one-bedroom basement apartment was simple but cozy. Exactly what I needed. It had new, plush, beige carpeting. And a spacious island counter that separated the combined kitchen

5 | A NEW HOME

and living room. And small, crank-style windows lined the top of the walls.

Rick threw a wadded paper towel in my direction as he cleaned the stove.

"This is dirty, brother!"

"It's good enough for what I need right now."

"I understand. I just think if you're going to rent a place, you do it right. They should've cleaned it."

"I know what you mean. But it will be okay."

"Well, pack your stuff. When do you want to move?"

"As soon as possible. Could you help me?"

"Sure, brother. Just let me know when."

"How about Wednesday morning at ten o'clock?"

"Sounds good. I don't have to work until late afternoon."

Wednesday came. Rick and I fit all my belongings in the back of his pickup truck. We traveled twenty minutes to Solvay and unloaded everything at the new place in an hour.

Aaron visited me often at my new apartment. And he planned to move in with me in the springtime.

One night, as we sat in front of the television eating dinner together, we conversed about where we wanted to live next. We planned to find a larger place and live together, as the Solvay apartment was too small for us on a long-term basis.

"Aaron. What if we got a house?"

"You mean, rent one?"

"Yeah. Or buy. Or maybe Mom and Dad would be willing to buy one that we could rent out."

"That would be nice! I'm tired of renting from crappy landlords."

"Me too!"

We prayed.

A week passed, then I mentioned to Mom and Dad we wanted a house.

"Maybe that would be a good opportunity," said Dad. "I'll contact a realtor and see if we can look at some places. What do you think you want?"

"I'm thinking maybe a duplex. We could live in one side and rent the other side."

A New Home

Over the next two months, we explored houses in the University area. None were satisfactory. But soon an opportunity emerged. A duplex house constructed in 1960 became available on Miles Avenue.

An elderly Jewish woman greeted us at the back door.

"Please come in. It's a very nice place. You'll enjoy it."

The exterior was a bold green except for the white, vertical paneling on the second story in the front. Four picture windows covered the front façade: two on the first floor and two on the second.

Each apartment had two bedrooms and a bathroom upstairs. Downstairs, each side had a living room, kitchen, half-bathroom, and a back porch. And the left side, which Aaron and I claimed, had a family room in the back. Each side also had a bedroom in the basement.

"My husband recently passed. That's why I'm selling it. I don't need all this house anymore."

"Well, we're sorry to hear that," said Mom.

5 | A NEW HOME

"Well, we lived here a lot of years. Lots of memories. But I'm ready to move on now."

After the tour, we sat in the family room.

"Well, what do you guys think?" said Dad, as he stood in the doorway between the kitchen and family room.

"I think this is the one!" I said.

"I agree!" said Aaron. "I like it!"

―※―

As I helped Aaron prepare to move into my apartment in Solvay, I talked to one of his roommates, Jack, about the new house.

"Oh, dude! Are you sure you guys want to do this?"

"Yeah! It will be a nice opportunity. The house is already purchased!"

"I don't know, dude. You guys could end up living there with each other for the rest of your lives! You could die there!"

"Well, you're right! That could happen! But let's pray about it and see!"

I prayed in silence for a minute.

About seven years.

The Inner Voice.

"So, Jack? I think God is saying to me we'll live there for about seven years. Seven and a half. Something like that."

"Okay, dude. Whatever. I'm just saying!"

―※―

After a few years living in the house, I recalled the message The Inner Voice spoke to me in 1999 when John dropped me off at the intersection. ***You're going to live there someday!***

The house we lived in *was* the house God spoke to me about. I'd forgotten about the incident until that moment.

I ran to tell Aaron about it.

"God showed me we were going to live here."

I told him the whole story.

"Really? I didn't know this. Why didn't you tell me?"

"I forgot about it."

"Huh! Well, this happened to me too!"

"What do you mean?"

"One day while I was walking to work, I decided to go down Miles Avenue. I saw a two-tone house. The bottom half green and the top half white. I thought, 'Why would someone paint a house like that!?' And God spoke to me!"

"What did he say?"

"I heard, **Careful what you say! You may live there someday!**"

The Inner Voice.

He heard the same message!

"Wow! So, what did you do?"

"I wasn't sure what to think about it. I was like, 'Okay, God. I'm sorry. Whatever you want!'"

"Well, that's amazing!"

"So, this was all in God's plan!"

"Yes! Apparently so!"

And we lived in the house for exactly seven and a half years.

In 2002 Rick moved to Wyoming. We lost touch again. But we would reconnect again in the future.

5 | A NEW HOME

In the fall of 2007, Aaron moved to Washington, D.C., to begin a career in information technology. A year later, I moved to Philadelphia for a job as a rehabilitation counselor.

We haven't lived together since, but we talk every day, and we visit each other frequently. My twin is still my best friend.

And I know the years we shared together in our God-appointed home enhanced our brotherly friendship.

They were years with many fond memories. Many visits from family and friends. And there were the crazy moments—like the night Aaron accidentally locked himself out and cut his hand as he tried to break in.

As I think back on the fond memories of these years, the following question comes to mind.

What is the difference between a house and a home?

A house is a physical structure. But a house becomes a home when love and friendship are shared within its walls.

Looking Ahead and Back

EVERY DECEMBER I take time to reflect on the past year. I began this practice one cloudy December afternoon as I gazed out the kitchen window at the Miles Avenue duplex.

I reflected on the past year and a half—since the move. And I recalled the message God spoke to Aaron and me on separate occasions: *You're going to live there someday!*

Looking Ahead and Back

I look back, because I've learned every year contains events I never anticipate—many of which are exciting and meaningful. This gives me hope for the new year—to expect great things.

And I've learned every year contains divine messages that I am unable to fully comprehend until later—like the message I received at the intersection. Though I clearly heard that message, I didn't know what to make of it at the time. I couldn't imagine we'd live in that house.

My thoughts during these annual times of reflection usually sound like this.

A year ago, at this time, I would never have imagined the events that occurred this year.

Then, I make mental notes of all the wonderful things I didn't expect to happen.

How did God speak to me this year about the future?

I make mental notes of the times God spoke to me over the past year—through The Inner Voice, Unexpected Grace, The Manifest Presence, The Visual Voice, through the voices of others, through written messages, and through dreams. And I'm inspired to continue listening for the Spirit's guidance in each moment.

What will next year bring?

We can only make such connections, however, when, in our everyday lives, we are alert to the Spirit. And regardless of how well we understand the messages in the moment we receive them, if we've taken time to listen, we can often put the pieces together during future reflection.

5 | A NEW HOME

A Woven Tapestry

I come away from these annual times of reflection with a deep sense of gratitude—for the past and the future. These moments ground me. They help make times of suffering and heartbreak more manageable by reminding me that ". . . all things work together for good for those who love God, for those who are called according to his purpose" (Romans 8:28 WEB).

Perhaps you've noticed I like *The Passion Translation.* Look how beautifully the same verse is written in that version!

> So we are convinced that every detail of our lives is continually woven together to fit into God's perfect plan of bringing good into our lives, for we are his lovers who have been called to fulfill his designed purpose.
>
> —ROMANS 8:28 TPT[4]

Every detail of our lives is continually woven into the tapestry of God's perfect plan. This means *all* that happens is meaningful!

Times of suffering *and* times of peace.
Times of lack *and* times of abundance.
Times of loneliness *and* times of befriending and love.

When God Is Silent

Looking ahead and back puts things in perspective. But there is one mode of being—one existential state—that is less tolerable than all others: when God is silent!

In such times, we are unable to derive meaning from our present and past experiences. And in pondering the future, we're unable to grasp a sense of direction or purpose.

Martin Luther once cried out, "Bless us, oh Lord; yea, even curse us, but please be not silent!" (Zacharias 1997, 67, par. 5).[5] Luther's words capture well, the pain of silence.

Job prayed similar words. He said, "I cry to you, and you do not answer me. I stand up, and you gaze at me" (Job 30:20 WEB). Was it something Job did that caused him not to hear? Or was there another reason?

The Book of Job clarifies he was blameless and upright, feared God, and shunned evil[6]—and that God allowed Satan to test him.[7] According to the epilogue, Job survived the hardship and silence, and God blessed the rest of his life.[8]

In Job's case, God's silence was not due to his wrongdoing but to test and reveal his faithfulness and God's character through him. God will prevail in our suffering.

At other times, God is silent during human persecution. For example, Jesus remained silent when the Sanhedrin falsely accused him in order to justify killing him. Matthew 26:62-63 states, "The high priest stood up and said to him, 'Have you no answer? What is this that these testify against you?' But Jesus stayed silent. The high priest answered him, 'I adjure you by the living God that you tell us whether you are the Christ, the Son of God.'"

And even Jesus endured God's silence—during his crucifixion. As the Bible tells, on that day, "For three hours, beginning at noon, darkness came over the earth. And at three o'clock Jesus shouted with a mighty voice in Aramaic, 'Eli, Eli,

5 | A NEW HOME

lema sabachthani?'—that is, 'My God, My God, why have you deserted me?'" (Matthew 27:45-46 TPT).[9]

God can seem distant when we hinder or block His voice. At other times, He is purposely silent. And there are times we do not know the reason for silence.

Regardless, silence is an integral part of our human and spiritual experience. When we accept this fact, we can appreciate it. In silence, there are usually opportunities for growth.

Meaning through Hardship

It is natural to derive meaning from our experiences. Austrian psychiatrist and Holocaust survivor, Viktor Frankl, believed finding meaning in life is the main motivation of humankind.[10] And developmental psychologist Robert Kegan asserted that being human is synonymous with meaning-making.[11]

Educational critics Neil Postman and Charles Weingartner used the term *meaning-making* to emphasize that learning is a creative process unique to each individual.[12] American psychologist George Kelly, the father of clinical psychology, shared this view.[13]

However, in cases of trauma, violence, or disaster, meaning-making and optimism may seem impossible—even heartless or disingenuous. But we can recover and grow after horrible circumstances.

This is called *posttraumatic growth*.

Outcomes of posttraumatic growth include meaningful relationships, new priorities, and an enhanced spiritual life.[14]

British psychologists Alex Linley and Stephen Joseph, in a 2004 review of thirty-nine studies of trauma survivors, suggested 30 to 70 percent of survivors experience posttraumatic growth.[15]

We can trust God to carry us through hardship. It may take time, patience, and support, but we can emerge on the other side—of silence, the wilderness, darkness, tragedy—with strengthened faith, rekindled hope, and new purpose.

Theoretical physicist Richard Feyman once wrote, "Nature uses only the longest threads to weave her patterns, so that each small piece of her fabric reveals the organization of the entire tapestry" (Feyman 2017, 34).[16] So it is, in spirit, as in physics!

We may neither understand the reasons for our circumstances, the meaning of the messages we receive, nor acquire direction for the future as quickly as we'd like, but we can rest assured the long thread, held firmly in the Weaver's hand, stitches every detail of our lives into a beautiful tapestry.

When we grasp this, we'll have more peace as we navigate our journeys. We'll be able to say with Job, "Though he slay me, yet will I hope in him" (Job 13:15a NIV),[17] and with Paul, "all things work together for good" (Romans 8:28 WEB).

Summary

As we open our hearts to listen and receive, we'll notice the many ways God speaks to us—if we're patient.

We'll more clearly hear God speak to our hearts—through the *still small voice*[18] and the voices of our friends, family, and lover. In the images we see by day and in our nighttime dreams.

5 | A NEW HOME

In the words we read. In nature—a sunrise, a bird's call, a pet's loving greeting. Through Grace and the Spirit. And in silence!

Looking ahead and back becomes a prophetic endeavor when we mix prayer, listening, and practice. We'll receive clarification about the past and hints about the future.

And, sometimes, we'll receive urgent messages that require immediate action, like in the story you'll read next.

On one, blustery winter night in 2003, The Inner Voice commanded me to **Go home immediately!**

6. SUNDAY NIGHT VOICES

The very voices of the night, sounding like the moan of the tempest, may turn out to be the disguised yet tender "voices of God," calling away from all earthly footsteps, to mount with greater singleness of eye and ardor of aim the alone ladder of safety and peace upward, onward, heavenward, homeward.

—John Ross Macduff [1]

A BLIZZARD RAGED outside, the winter of 2003 fully upon us. Syracuse winters were always brutal, but we were used to them, having grown up in Central New York. However, one night caught us off guard.

Aaron had a mobile phone. I did not. We mostly relied on our landline connection and retrieved messages from the answering machine upon arriving home. We couldn't communicate about urgent matters as quickly as we can today.

Home alone and hungry, with an empty fridge, I donned my heavy fur coat and boots to trek the ten-minute walk to Rite Aid. A trip we were accustomed to making between larger food trips to Peter's Groceries.

As I stepped outside under the royal blue sky, snow glistened in the orange glow of the streetlights. I glance up Miles Avenue. The air was powdery, and visibility was poor.

Maybe I shouldn't do this.

Nah. Should be okay.

Trudging through the southeast sidewalks, the trip took longer than usual.

When I arrived at Nottingham Plaza, I glanced across the dimly lit parking lot. I peered into the darkened store windows. Everything was closed.

Oh! It's Sunday night! Rite Aid closes at six on Sunday!

I sighed. The fridge at home was still empty.

I guess I'll order out.

I clutched the ruff of my Akademiks fur coat, drawing it snugly around my face. Thirty percent fox. Good to thirty below! An item I purchased two years prior that made walking in these conditions easier and safer.

─────⋆⋅☆⋅⋆─────

Just then, The Inner Voice spoke—more strongly than usual. Insistent!

Go home immediately!

Is that just my thoughts?

6 | SUNDAY NIGHT VOICES

The voice came again, with a feeling of pressure in my chest and a sense of urgency.

Go home! Now!

Aaron came to mind.

Is Aaron in trouble?

I ignored such promptings in the past yet later realized their validity. I turned to walk, but then I ran.

I sped as fast as I could through the powdery streets. Halfway, out of breath, I slipped and fell.

Is there really a reason to run?

I stood and walked ten steps, regaining my energy. Then I ran the rest of the way.

The front light illuminated the night as I jogged to the front door.

I paused.

Nothing.

Okay. Well, better safe than sorry.

I stepped toward the door, anxious to get out of the cold.

But in the darkness to my left, I heard rustling.

Footsteps.

A voice.

"I've got a real problem!"

I glanced left. Aaron paced toward me from the back corner of the house.

He must have come home while I was out.

"What's wrong!?" I said, my mouth and eyes widening.

"I locked myself out and I tried to get in! I cut myself!" His right arm shook.

"How!?" I said.

"I tried to get in through the back-porch glass louvers and one broke!"

His hand bled. We needed to get inside immediately. I tried to remain calm as I unlocked the door.

"We might need to go to the hospital!" Aaron said.

"Well, let's look at it first," I said. "Come up here to the sink," I said, ascending the stairs before him.

Holding Aaron's arm in the bathroom sink, I applied my first aid training from Boy Scouts and counseling school.

I calmed myself.

Deep breath.

I slowly turned on the tap, washing away enough blood to see the depth of the cut.

"Hmm. It doesn't look too bad," I said. "But I think you're gonna need stitches."

We glanced at each other.

"Well, we need to get it bandaged, at least," I said, opening the drawer of Band-Aids Aaron stocked a year prior.

We sat in the kitchen with Aaron's bandaged hand. From the windowsill, an electric Christmas candle spread its soft light across the room.

We contemplated how to get to the hospital. The injury didn't seem urgent enough for an ambulance, and we both couldn't drive because of low vision.[2]

"We could call John," I said.

"We could."

"Alright. Let's try," I said.

John answered.

6 | SUNDAY NIGHT VOICES

"Aaron got locked out and tried to break in through the back-porch glass louvers and cut his hand," I said. "We need someone to drive him to the hospital."

"I could probably do it. But it might take me a bit. The weather is really bad. Give me like twenty minutes."

"Okay. That's fine. See you in a bit."

I hung up the phone.

We waited.

John drove slowly through the snow-hampered streets, as Aaron sat in the passenger's seat and I sat in the back.

We arrived at University Hospital. Its emergency entrance perched oddly on the hillside, and the greenish glow of the waiting room shone into the trepid night.

Aaron disappeared into the examination area as John and I sat in the waiting room. It had been a while since we talked.

The conversation turned to laughter. And time itself stretched beyond the hospital walls, morphing our words into elongated, tired rhythms.

"I wonder what's taking so long," I finally said.

"I don't know," said John. "There's really not a lot of people here."

"How long have we been sitting here?"

"Probably an hour. Maybe more."

"I'm not really surprised."

"Oh, there he is!" I said. "Did you get stitches?"

"I did," said Aaron. "But the doctor was rude."

I cocked my head. "What?

"He saw my hand and said, 'Is that all!?'"

"Uh! That's ridiculous."

"That is rude," John chuckled. "But you're okay now?"

"Well, there was someone screaming in the room next to me," said Aaron. "Did you hear that?"

"No," I said. "But still. That's rude."

"Yeah, I'm okay now. Let's go."

We arrived home around ten o'clock. Aaron and I sat in the kitchen, discussing the night's events, the Christmas candle again shining its hopeful light in the darkness.

"I heard a voice tell me to go home immediately. I ran!"

"What!? Wow! Well, good thing you did!" said Aaron. "I wasn't sure what I was gonna do. I thought maybe I would be out there all night!"

"I'm glad I came back when I did!"

"Where were you!?" said Aaron.

"I went to Rite Aid."

"Why? It's Sunday night!"

"Yeah, I know," I said. "I forgot they're closed this late on Sunday."

"Well, I'm sure glad you came back when you did," said Aaron. "Any later and I would've lost more blood."

"I'm sorry," I said, glancing down at the table.

"Well, it's taken care of now," said Aaron. "But we need a better plan if we get locked out in the future."

"I agree."

We ordered dinner.

6 | SUNDAY NIGHT VOICES

An Open Heart

NOT ALL THE voices we hear are worth listening to. Especially those that tear down our self-worth. Yet, others are essential to heed, as this story shows. Discerning the voices is crucial and can even save lives.

The voice of God is disguised to those with untrained ears, but familiar to those who believe and heed its direction.

To hear and follow, we must cultivate an open heart. Doing so is like tending a garden, which needs good soil, well-planted seeds, ample water, and sunlight.

To grow spiritually, we must resolve the barriers to hearing and responding—on a spiritual level. We must relinquish our pride, heal the pain of our past, and practice listening.

Pride

There is a cost to developing spiritual hearing. Our ego and pride stand in the way.

We must first acknowledge there is something—someone—greater than ourselves. A Creator, with whom we can pursue a relationship.

Doing so requires faith—believing in what we cannot see. Hebrews 11:6 (NIV) states, "And without faith it is impossible to please God, because anyone who comes to him must believe he exists and that he rewards those who earnestly seek him."[3]

And even after we learn to listen, our pride can stand in the way of acting on what we hear, with rationalizations like,

"That's just my thoughts!" or "I can't do that!" or "It would be embarrassing to say that!"

In order to heed the messages God speaks to us, however, we must value the message more than our comfort.

And we can when we know how much God loves us. After all, it's quite difficult to obey someone we distrust. But let God pour love into you and your doubts will fade.

That love will change you! You'll develop a passion for responding to His voice! Your love for yourself and others will grow. You'll begin to see life in a whole new way!

Pain

Holding on to emotional wounds from our past can make trusting God difficult. But when we open our hearts to the Spirit, we experience love and healing.

We hear our first sounds as early as eighteen weeks in utero, after which our hearing capacity continues to grow.[4]

Research shows when developing fetuses hear their mother's voice—and other maternal sounds—from the womb, their auditory cortex thickens bilaterally, resulting in enhanced auditory capacity after birth.[5]

And the first voice we hear *after* birth is our mother's—unless we are born without the capacity to hear. And even without hearing, we can communicate with our caregiver(s) through our other senses.

Research has repeatedly shown that healthy attachment in infancy is the *sine qua non* for healthy brain development—and emotional and social functioning.[7] A quality, loving bond between the parent or parental figure—especially mother—and infant is essential.

The voices of our father and siblings are also among the first voices we hear after birth—if we are fortunate enough to have them present. Research shows children who live with their biological parents fare better physically, emotional, and academically.[8] Conversely, instability—in family structure, income, housing, and community—negatively impacts children's development.[9]

Unstable and abusive environments are full of punitive voices. Children repeat the voices they hear whether nurturing or destructive. And absorbing punitive messages ultimately leads to self-doubt and depression.[10] At worst, in chaotic family systems, children acquire trauma from abuse or neglect. And when trauma is internalized and unresolved, it often invades other life aspects.

Family trauma—and its associated voices—is both verbal and nonverbal. Intergenerational trauma expert Mark Wolynn explains that the *core language* of trauma can manifest as "physical sensations, behaviors, emotions, impulses, and even the symptoms of an illness" (Wolynn 2016, 53).[11]

Judith Pickering, an Australian psychoanalytic couple therapist, Jungian analyst, and psychotherapist, explains that transgenerational trauma can manifest in our dreams. She wrote that "unresolved intergenerational trauma may be transmitted through unconscious channels of communication, manifesting in the dreams of descendants" (Pickering 2012, 576).[12] And the voices of trauma replicate themselves across the generations, continuing the cycle until it is broken.

Trauma survivors learn to distrust the voices they hear—their own and others'. Fortunately, healing is possible—through psychotherapy, mindfulness-based techniques, caring relationships, and spiritual connection.

For some people, connection to the Divine is the first loving relationship they've had. And if you doubt such a relationship is possible, consider the many available stories. YouTube is full of salvation and angelic rescue stories. If you've never taken the time to watch them, I encourage you to do so. Regardless of your history—whether nurturing or traumatic, religious or irreligious, spiritual or unspiritual—the plethora of amazing testimonies should pique your curiosity. There truly is someone greater involved in our journeys!

Overcoming distrust incurred through hurt and pain, however, can initially make embracing a loving God difficult. But when we open our hearts to the truth beyond ourselves, love pours in. And the future looks much brighter.

King David wrote the following, expressed beautifully in *The Passion Translation*.

> You've gone into my future to prepare the way, and in kindness you follow behind me to spare me from the harm of my past. With your hand of love upon my life, you impart a blessing to me.
>
> —PSALM 139:5 TPT[13]

And as the Bible shows, God knew us before conception and has a plan for each of us. Surely, we have a reason to examine what this means for our lives.

The prophet Jeremiah wrote the following words God spoke to him. "Before I formed you in the womb, I knew you.

Before you were born, I sanctified you. I have appointed you a prophet to the nations" (Jeremiah 1:5 WEB).

And Jesus reminded his disciples of their worth and encouraged them not to worry. He said to them, "Aren't five sparrows sold for two assaria coins? Not one of them is forgotten by God. But the very hairs of your head are all counted. Therefore don't be afraid. You are of more value than many sparrows" (Luke 12:6-7).

In ancient Rome, the *assarion*, or *as*, was a small copper coin similar to a penny.[14] A half *as* could buy a loaf of bread; one *as* could buy a liter of wine.[15] According to the *World English Bible*, one assaria coin was pay for an hour of agricultural labor.[16]

But you? You're worth many *asses*! You're priceless!

Practice

The stories you've read so far emphasize spiritual hearing. It may seem anecdotal, then, to mention we also hear physically. But both are important. Practicing physical listening can enhance spiritual listening, and vice versa.

Suffice it to say, most people can hear well physically. But fewer people are adept at listening well. And even fewer people develop spiritual hearing. Yet, this is possible for everyone.

Listening—at any level—takes practice. And patience!

Mindful listening is a practice that can enhance our skills at both levels. John Kabat-Zinn, mindfulness teacher and professor emeritus (University of Massachusetts Medical School) explained that mindfulness is about purposeful, nonjudgmental attention in the present moment.[17] He further explained that practicing mindful listening enhances our awareness, sense of clarity, and acceptance of reality.[18]

As you cultivate your listening skills, I encourage you to remember the three P's. *Pride*, *Pain*, and *Practice*. We must deal with our pride which blocks faith, heal the pain of our past in order to trust fully and freely, and practice listening.

Life—and I say this from personal experience—truly becomes exciting when we open our hearts and begin listening. Yes, in a deeper way to each other, but also to the Spirit.

Summary

The following words of John Ross Macduff capture the meaning of my experience. The voice during the nighttime storm turned out to be the loving voice of God calling me homeward.

> The very voices of the night, sounding like the moan of the tempest, may turn out to be the disguised yet tender "voices of God," calling away from all earthly footsteps, to mount with greater singleness of eye and ardor of aim the alone ladder of safety and peace upward, onward, heavenward, homeward.[19]

I am grateful I heeded the Spirit's prompting and rescued my brother. Thorough inner work refined the state of my heart and prepared me to hear and respond.

7. EXTERNAL VOICES

No one is useless in this world who lightens the burdens of it for anyone else.

—Charles Dickens [1]

SEPTEMBER 2003 MARKED the start of a new venture for me—a master of counseling degree at Syracuse University. I was ready for a change—after spending eight long years working in food services and grocery stores.

At the beginning of the school year, the Department of Counseling and Human Services hosted their annual picnic for incoming graduate students. The picnic was held at Clark

Reservation State Park in Jamesville, just five miles south of Syracuse. A beautiful park. The New York State Parks, Recreation and Historic Preservation website states it is "a geologic wonder of the last ice age and a botanist's paradise" (2019).[2]

At the center of the park is Glacier Lake—a sixty-five-foot-deep *glacial plunge pool lake*—formed by an ancient waterfall. The lake sits in a 165-foot-deep gorge, accessible only by a 175-step stone staircase. And surrounding the lake, limestone cliffs reach up to 185 feet.[3]

Glacier Lake is a rare type, a *meromictic lake*, of which there are less than fifty in the world, with four located in New York State—Irondequoit Bay in Rochester, Ballston Lake in Albany, and Green Lake and Glacier Lake in Syracuse area.[4]

In meromictic lakes, the surface and underlying waters do not mix because the lake's steep sides and narrow surface area cause separate water layers to form, each with unique aquatic environments.[5]

Clark Reservation is also home to the largest population in the United States of a rare, endangered fern. The American Hart's Tongue (*Asplenium scolopendrium*).[6]

The park is a geologic wonder and a botanist's paradise for sure, but also dangerous if one isn't careful.

∞

On Saturday morning at eleven o'clock, Kaylee drove up with Rachael in the passenger's seat. I trotted across the front lawn, acknowledging it's need for a few more cuts before the cold. I hopped in the back seat.

We headed south, past the duck pond and through Barry Park. Over Colvin Street and past the Syracuse University

7 | EXTERNAL VOICES

Athletic Complex. Down the long stretch of Comstock Avenue. Over Thurber Street to East Brighton Avenue. And into the rolling hills of East Seneca Turnpike, to Clark Reservation.

The three of us, all new graduate students just getting to know each other, conversed about the upcoming school year, our classes, and who we expected to show for the picnic.

Kaylee made a left turn into the park, and another left.

"Is this right?"

"We should've gone straight," I said. "This is the office."

"Oh, yeah. You're right."

She turned around, made a left, and drove until we saw the parking booth marked "CLARK RESERVATION," the long lot beyond it, and Glacier Lake glimmering through the trees.

As we exited the car we continued our conversation.

"Did you see Dr. Gilroy's PowerPoint error?" said Kaylee.

"What error?" I said. "When?"

"Oh! You mean 'In pubic!?'" Rachael butted in.

"Yeah, Rachael. That one! Tuesday night's class!"

"I saw that! I bet he did that on purpose. Just took the L out of 'public' to see how we'd react!"

"Oh, my gawd! You mean, like, to test us?" said Kaylee.

"Yeah! Like a psychological experiment!" I said.

"Ha-ha! You're probably right!"

"What was that supposed to say?" said Rachael.

"It was supposed to be 'in public rehabilitation.'"

"Well, that's not what he wrote!" I said.

We silenced our laughter as we walked across the grass to the pavilion where staff and students gathered.

"'In pubic.' I can't believe it," I whispered. "Probably just an honest mistake."

"Yeah right," Kaylee whispered back. "Shhhhh!"

⁂

Kaylee asked our department head whether we could take a hike through the surrounding trails, which she knew well. She granted Kaylee's request. And Kaylee, Rachael, Jake, and I set out toward the woods.

We hiked east on Mildred Faust Woodland Trail. For a while, I heard the voices of our classmates at the pavilion below.

"Oh, wait!" said Kaylee. "I think we're going the wrong way. We need to get on another trail that goes over by the lake. There's a really cool spot with a beautiful view."

We climbed to Cliff Trail through steep, slippery rocks and roots and hiked north. The trees, still green, at times blocked the view ahead.

"What time do you plan on heading back," I said.

"Why?" said Kaylee. "Do you have a hot date?"

"No! I wish!"

"You can admit it! I'll give you a ride home if you need it."

"I don't. But a ride home would be nice."

"Sure."

"I was just asking how long you plan on hiking, here."

"Oh. Probably just like thirty minutes or something."

"How often do you come here, Kaylee?" said Jake.

"I haven't been up here in a while. But my family comes here sometimes. We did a lot more when I was younger."

"Do they know where we are?" said Rachel.

"Who?" said Kaylee.

"Everyone! Our classmates."

7 | EXTERNAL VOICES

"Oh! I just told Dr. Burton. She knows."

I kept my eyes on the ground to avoid tripping.

The trail curved left.

"Stop!"

The External Voice.

I stopped in my tracks and jolted my head up. Less than ten feet ahead of me was a steep cliff. And Glacier Lake below.

I glanced to my left a split second later and saw Kaylee's arm outstretched, her palm facing me.

"If you didn't just say something, I would have gone right off that cliff!" I said, my heart racing. "How did you know!?"

"I don't know! I just thought of your eyesight and wondered if you'd see it."

My eyesight does pose some limitations. But in this case I didn't see the cliff because I watched my feet to avoid tripping.

We hiked to where we could view the lake, and there, we took a break, enjoying the view, the sunlight, and the breeze.

Then we began our return to the pavilion.

"Well. Let's see. What happened today? We had a picnic. We hiked. Kaylee saved my life!"

"Do you still need a ride home?" Kaylee chuckled.

I grinned. "Well, now that I'm still alive! Yes!"

Lighten the Burdens

CHARLES DICKENS WROTE, "No one is useless in this world who lightens the burdens of it for someone else" (Dickens [1864-1865] 1997, 492).[7]

Dickens's character, Bella Wilfer, spoke these words in *Our Mutual Friend*.[8]

Bella is somewhat vain, and admits to it, but as the story progresses, she humbles and even depreciates herself.

In response to her self-depreciation, Mr. Boffin's secretary, Mr. Rokesmith—actually the supposedly deceased John Harmon—comforts Bella with the above words.

Like Bella, we're sometimes distracted by our sense of self-importance or lack of it. Like Bella, we need reminders that what matters most are our acts of love and kindness.

It's difficult to heed God's promptings to lighten another's burdens when we're preoccupied with ourselves. But as we relinquish our pride, we can respond more freely.

I certainly count Kaylee's act of saving me from injury or death as *lightening the burdens.*

As we help others, we're often aware of our impact—such as through our chosen profession. We know our impact through our actions and through occasional feedback. In the same way, we know our impact on our family and friends.

At other times, God works through us despite our lack of knowledge. We learn of our helpfulness later, either directly from the people we unknowingly helped or through other means.

And we won't know all the ways we've blessed people—at least in this lifetime. The Bible shows that we're often unaware of our impact.

See the following words Jesus spoke about the final judgment. He also explains that the way we treat others is how we treat God!

7 | EXTERNAL VOICES

> Then the King will tell those on his right hand, "Come, blessed of my Father, inherit the Kingdom prepared for you from the foundation of the world; for I was hungry and you gave me food to eat. I was thirsty and you gave me drink. I was a stranger and you took me in. I was naked and you clothed me. I was sick and you visited me. I was in prison and you came to me."
>
> Then the righteous will answer him, saying, "Lord, when did we see you hungry and feed you, or thirsty and give you a drink? When did we see you as a stranger and take you in, or naked and clothe you? When did we see you sick or in prison and come to you?"
>
> The King will answer them, "Most certainly I tell you, because you did it to one of the least of these my brothers, you did it to me."
>
> —MATTHEW 25:34–40 WEB

According to the Bible, the angels are watching too! The author of the Book of Hebrews, likely Paul the Apostle, wrote the following.

> No matter what, make room in your heart to love every believer. And show hospitality to strangers, for they may be angels from God showing up as your guests. Identify with those who are in prison as though you were there suffering with them, and those who are mistreated as if you could feel their pain.
>
> —HEBREWS 13:1–3 TPT[9]

I didn't know Kaylee's standing with God, but I did know she was from a Catholic family. Regardless, God used her to spare my life. Instead of tumbling off Cliff Trail and down an almost vertical embankment into Glacier Lake, I made it home that evening alive.

Kaylee didn't intentionally rescue me. She spontaneously responded to an internal prompting. A split-second response. She yelled, "*Stop!*" as she extended her arm and the palm of her hand. She startled me into a dead standstill!

It did not have to happen that way. She could have ignored the prompting; I could have dismissed her warning. I often wonder how many times I *have* missed crucial moments due to my pride and stubbornness, neurotic self-absorption, or lack of attention. Thinking about this encourages me to tune my inner ear to the Spirit—whether in the form of The Inner Voice, Unexpected Grace, The Manifest Presence, The Visual Voice, or The External Voice.

And it is intriguing to me that I received no inner prompting as I approached the cliff. It instead came from outside—Kaylee's voice. In my experience, that is just how it goes sometimes. God works through each of us to help each other—in addition to communicating with us internally.

Do you value the voices of others? If not, you're likely to end up in peril.

In non-threatening situations, we have time to discern and respond to external voices. But in emergencies, such as my cliff experience, there is no time to think. Only react.

Therefore, it is crucial to develop our spiritual hearing so we can heed the promptings that come to us.

7 | EXTERNAL VOICES

We cannot control when they come. And to me, that makes life with the Spirit challenging and exciting.

Are you listening?

And will you act when prompted?

Will you be The External Voice to another in need?

Will you lighten the burdens?

8. NO ORDINARY CAT

Above all the grace and the gifts that Christ gives to his beloved is that of overcoming self.

—St. Francis of Assisi [1]

S**HE WAS MOTIONLESS.** I was scared and I didn't know what to do. I picked her up and stood her on her feet. She attempted to walk but she fell. Then she dragged herself to the refrigerator indicating hunger. And though I fed her she ate little. My heart sank.

Fortunately, I wasn't alone. Aaron flew in from Washington, D.C. to visit me for the weekend.

Saturday, March 13, 2010 was sunny and bright, but we wouldn't enjoy it.

"Aaron!?"

He was still asleep.

"Aaron!?" I called, louder.

"What?" he mumbled.

"Um. We have a problem!"

"Oh, no. What do you mean?"

"Please come here!"

"Why?"

"Something's wrong!"

A beautiful, year-long relationship would soon have a sad ending.

• • •

I walked into Joy's office. It was September 25, 2009.

"Have you seen Shana?"

"She's still outside with the cat."

"Oh, yeah. I heard about that."

"I'm not gonna bother her. There's no convincing her to come back up here this afternoon. That's how she is with stuff like this."

"Huh! Maybe I need to go check this out!"

"Well, have fun dear! But what did you need?"

"There's a case folder she has that I need."

"Well, good luck getting it today!"

"Ha-ha. That's fine. I'm gonna go see the cat."

"Fill me in on the details!"

I walked out of my supervisor's office, down the main hallway, and through the glass doors leading to the waiting room of the Office of Vocational Rehabilitation.

8 | NO ORDINARY CAT

I boarded the elevator to the ground floor.

Outside, the sun shone through a clear sky. And there, in front of the building Shana and Nate stood, peering into a box.
"What's in there!?"
"Oh! Did Joy tell you!?" said Shana.
"Yeah. But I heard you talking about it earlier."
From within the box, a beautiful gray cat stared up at me.
I reached in.
"Careful!" said Shana. "She's not in too good a mood. She's been in this box for an hour! She or he! We don't know yet."
I reached in. The cat hissed and I drew back my hand.
"So, what are you gonna do?" I said.
"Well, Carrie took her someplace to check if she has a microchip."
"And?"
"Nothing. Do you want a cat for the night, Nate?"
"I can't. I have allergies. I could put her in the basement overnight. But I don't think that's such a good idea."
"Do you want a cat, Jason? Lynn would give you a ride."
"Wow. I mean. It would be hard to resist. I don't know."

Five o'clock came and I found myself in the back of Lynn's car with the cat. Shana sat in the passenger's seat, frequently looking back to check on the situation.

I again attempted to pet the cat. More hissing and growling commenced, but then the cat relaxed, seeming grateful for the attention.

I now have a cat!

FROM BEYOND THE VEIL

We arrived at my Hoffman Street rowhouse in South Philly. And as I carried the cat-filled box to the door, I felt both excited and nervous.

Five minutes later, I headed out again—to Andrew Grocery. A little convenient store at the corner of Fourth and McKean. There amidst the dusty shelves I located a disposable litter box, bowls, and cans of cat food.

I returned home and put out the litter box, food, and water in the corner of the kitchen. The cat ate and pooped—and then hid for the night behind the toilet in the upstairs bathroom.

In the weeks that followed, I built a trusting relationship with my new friend.

I discovered she especially went crazy for Pounce treats!

And a vet visit revealed she needed medication, which I administered faithfully for two weeks.

The cat turned out to be female. A Russian Blue.

I named her Clawdia.

Soon, my family met her.

Everyone loved her.

———

A month passed since the day I rescued Clawdia.

I awoke with a start.

What is today? Sunday.

I took a deep breath and reflected on the vivid dream I just awoke from.

I was in a stone-lined tunnel. And at its end was a bright light. The most powerful sense of love I'd ever felt emanated from the light source.

Ahead of me, Clawdia floated through the tunnel toward the light. I followed behind her, observing.

8 | NO ORDINARY CAT

A voice came from the light, saying, ***"Treat her well. It's one of the most important things you will do."***

Pondering its nature, I recognized the dream as prophetic, presented by The Divine Cinematographer onto the projection screen of perception.[2]

Prophetic dreams contain divine messages. They come with a sense of clarity that other dreams do not have. Their events seem hyperreal. And they come with a sense of knowing that they're about the future.[3]

I've received many prophetic dreams over the years, but something intrigued me about this one. The message that caring for Clawdia would be one of the most important tasks given me in this lifetime.

How could this be?

I thought of all the important things I've accomplished. Counseling people, music ministry, helping friends and family, and more. But I knew God spoke through the dream, and I resolved not to question the authority presented within it.

God, I will take care of Clawdia. I promise. You have my word!

⸻

In January of 2010, eager to leave my South Philly rowhouse which became roach infested, I packed my belongings. My destination? A rowhouse in Northeast Philly.

Clawdia appeared confused at all my belongings filling the living room. She had a traumatic past, and I worried this made it worse. I felt sad as I observed her perched atop my rug, now rolled up in the center of the room.

"We're going to a new place!"

I spoke to her in a calm, high-pitch voice.

"Okay? It'll be okay. I love you!"

She coked her head.

⁂

One evening, I set out a bowl of ice cream for myself on the floor in front of the television. Then, after returning from the kitchen to retrieve a spoon, I saw Clawdia lapping vanilla ice cream from the bowl.

"No!" I scolded.

She hid under the kitchen table.

I recalled my dream and immediately felt horrible.

I hurried to the kitchen, picked her up in my arms, and carried her to the living room. I slumped into the couch, hugging her until she purred, desperate to maintain our loving bond.

⁂

Aaron came to visit me in Northeast Philly for the weekend. It was his second visit since I rescued Clawdia and he was happy to see her.

The following morning, Saturday, March 13, 2010, was the sad day I woke to find she couldn't walk.

I spent the morning locating an emergency clinic. The only option available on the weekend was Veterinary Specialty and Emergency Center, twenty minutes northeast of my apartment.

The light faded from the sky as dusk fell. And pouring rain pelted the windshield. Aaron and I sat in the back seat, and I held Clawdia, in her carrier, on my lap.

The cab driver lost his way, extending the trip well beyond twenty minutes. Then, when we arrived, we waited another thirty minutes for the veterinarian.

8 | NO ORDINARY CAT

We left.
A silent cab ride home.
I walked up the steps, Aaron following behind.
I turned the key in the lock then paused.
"Well, Aaron. This has been a sad day."
"It's not the same. No Clawdia."
"Nope. It's not the same."
"Feels empty."
"It is."

We arose late on Sunday.
"What are we doing for lunch?" said Aaron.
"Do you wanna go out somewhere?"
"Sure. But what would be open on Sunday?"
"Yeah. Good point."
I grabbed my phone and searched for places.
"There is an Asian place nearby I've never been too. It's like a Chinese and Japanese combination restaurant."
"Hmm. Is it any good?"
"Well, the reviews don't look great. But there isn't much else open. Unless you want Wendy's."
"No. Let's try the Asian place."

A tall waiter with dark hair and sunken eyes greeted us.
"Two?"
"Yes, just two."
He led us across the dingy restaurant to a table and we sat.
"The table is sticky!"

"That's not a good sign."
"The menus are too."
We looked over the menu.
"What are you getting?"
"Hmm. I think I'm getting a bento box," I said. "What are you getting?
"I'm getting the combination platter."

⚭

Our plates arrived.
"Aaron, look at this! The bento box literally came in a wood box. This looks well used."
"It's actually a wooden box?"
I dug in. The food was bland.
"I think I lost my appetite."
"Mine is okay," said Aaron. "Not great!"
I opened my fortunate cookie. Nothing memorable.
"What does yours say?"
He opened his cookie
"Um. You're not gonna believe this!"
"What!?"
"Well. Look at it."
He handed me the paper.
"There's no such thing as an ordinary cat."
A piece of the Divine Script!

⚭

I bought a shadow box. Dad hung Clawdia's clay footprint inside of it for me, and underneath, the special message from the cookie.
There truly is no such thing as an ordinary cat!

Spontaneous Selflessness

CLAWDIA CAME INTO my life for a reason and a season. I initiated the relationship by choosing to take her home. But, in another sense, she chose me. And behind the scene The Divine Cinematographer planned it all.

Reflecting on this special time in my life posed important questions. I've only recently discovered the answers.

Why did God say that taking care of Clawdia would be one of my most important assignments? What lessons was I to learn from this? And why did God communicate through a dream and a fortune cookie?

Don't Prejudge: The Transitory

First, what I've come to understand is this. We think we know what is most important in our lives—and to God—but we're likely incorrect more than we realize. We must learn to accept rather than prejudge our impact and experiences.

There are some concrete things we do know, and then there are the gray areas—where we improvise. We decide what is most important. A best guess. And a lot gets mixed into this gray area. Family values, cultural norms, and much more. Some of these beliefs and ideas serve us well. Others do not.

I imagine many of us would be uncomfortable knowing the full, unbridled truth about what was, is, and will be important in our lives. I suspect we'd be surprised to learn that much of what we think is important, isn't. And vice versa.

Therefore, we must not prejudge our impact by assuming the big things count and the little things don't. Or that the transitory moments—along our way to the tangible—are meaningless and futile.

Meeting, accepting, and caring for Clawdia was one of these moments, for me. I could've declined the opportunity. And I almost did! But I would've missed out on a big part of the Divine Script. So, I accepted the cat!

⁂

Often, it's in the *transitory* and *spontaneous* that we find the most meaning. Art and architecture show this quite well.

The French Impressionists of the nineteenth century valued and captured the transitory moments of contemporary, middle-class life, in depictions of landscape, leisure, and recreation, emphasizing the fleeting nature of light and movement—an opposition to the formal style of the prior century which drew mainly from history and mythology.[4]

French filmmaker, Jean Rouch (1917-2004), strongly influenced by Surrealism, often and deliberately depicted spontaneity and the chance encounter (*recontre*) in his films.[5] Rouch invented *cinéma vérité* ("truthful cinema"), a documentary style relying on improvisation and the camera operator's direct participation.[6]

And, more recently, American architect Julian Hunt, when speaking about revitalizing the abandoned railway station under Washington, D.C.'s Dupont Circle, expressed, "The accidental encounter—the opportunity to meet people from different places and different backgrounds—is what makes culture alive" (CGTN America 2015, 6:00).[7]

8 | NO ORDINARY CAT

Our lives are like architecture, art, and film—a creative space. And we have much leeway in how we use this space. But *how* we use our life space determines whether we'll live meaningful, joy-filled lives.

We can live in the past rather than appreciate the present, transitory, impressionistic moments. We can ignore the precious opportunities that stream our way as we hurry forward toward what we deem essential. But life isn't exciting that way.

Or we can choose, instead, to suspend our prejudgments as we value every moment as meaningful. In so doing, we gain access to all the magical stuff of life.

This endeavor becomes easier when we learn to value the Spirit's direction over our own agenda. Through practice, we'll cultivate spontaneity with The Divine Cinematographer. We'll more easily see the Divine Script playing in ours and others' living theaters; the Painter's hand upon the canvass; the Architect's intention in our spontaneous meetings.

And *this* makes for an exciting and meaningful life.

On Dreams: The Oneiric

We dream whether we're awake or asleep. And we're continuously connected to the dream world—from which ideas, inspiration, and creativity flow. Our lives are a constant *oneiric* (dreamlike) experience.[8] And the dream space isn't just psychic; it's joined to and interwoven with the spiritual.[9]

There are examples throughout the Bible of people who received messages in dreams. And there are contemporary examples. You'll be surprised to learn how many inventors received ideas in dreams. Take a look at the following list!

The automatic sewing machine (invented by Elias Howe); the chemical structure of benzene (Friedrich August Kekule Stradonitz); the periodic table (Dimitri Mendeleev); Lorenzo's Oil for treating adrenoleukodystrophy (Lorenzo Odone); insulin for treating diabetes (Paul Langerhans); *Book of Dreams* (Jack Kerouac); *Avatar* (James Cameron); *River of Dreams* (Billy Joel); *Rite of Spring* (by Igor Stravinsky).[10]

The shape of DNA (James Watson); the scientific method (René Descartes); the theory of relativity (Albert Einstein); *The Terminator* (James Cameron, again); *Inception* (Chris Nolan); *Yesterday* (The Beatles); Google (Larry Page).[11]

You can receive through dreams too, and if you're not, simply—but diligently—pray, "God, please reveal yourself to me in my dreams!"

Selflessness

The message in my dream was not that taking care of Clawdia was the most important thing I'll do, but that it would be *one* of the most important things I'll do.

Pondering this, I questioned what characteristics this and similar acts of kindness possess. After some thought, the answer came to me. What characterized my acceptance of Clawdia—and all similar deeds—was *selflessness*.

Our selfless acts that matter most!

Thus, my second realization. *Anytime* we act selflessly, it's the *most important thing* we'll do!

I've certainly not always acted selflessly. But, I do remember the times I have given despite myself—my interests,

8 | NO ORDINARY CAT

desires, feelings, and comfort. These moments were meaningful because they meant something to others.

My choosing to accept Clawdia was a selfless act.

At the time, doing so was inconvenient. I wasn't emotionally ready to care for an animal and I didn't have much extra money to do so.

Though I love cats and wanted one again, my main motivation wasn't for companionship. My motivation was to rescue Clawdia from a life of pain.

She came with a flea collar. But how long had she roamed the streets of Northern Liberties? And had she traveled from another Philly neighborhood? Further? Did she suffer at the hands of her previous owner? No one wanted to give her a home. I was the chosen one. I had to take her.

And though my time with Clawdia brought much happiness, it was not without difficulty. Though I budgeted well for food and litter, the visits to the veterinarian were costly. And my heart broke when she fell ill.

My concern was more for her than for myself.

Selfless, caring people share something in common, according to Kristen Renwick Monroe, an American political scientist who studies altruism. Through her interviews with many individuals who rescued Jews during World War II, she found altruistic people are ordinary, not heroic types. And the one crucial characteristic they shared was how they viewed others.[12]

She recalled that "when an altruist or rescuer looked at a stranger, they would just see another human being. They thought of themselves as people who were tied together, bonded together, to other people through the common humanity that we all shared" (Adler 2015, par. 17).[13]

We don't always have the chance to learn how we've helped, but when we do receive feedback about such moments, the value of our selfless acts becomes evident, positively reinforcing our future motivation to act with empathy, compassion, and kindness. Through my dream, God clearly communicated the importance of selflessness.

We must not assume living a selflessness life is easy, however. St. Francis of Assisi said, "Above all the grace and gifts Christ gives to his beloved is that of overcoming self" (Rhodes 2015, 197).[14] We should pray for this gift, for we cannot live a life of selfless love on human strength alone. We must rely on God's immeasurable grace!

Shared Selflessness

Why did The Divine Cinematographer speak to me in a dream—and follow it up with a piece of the Divine Script, placed in a fortune cookie and distributed to Aaron?

The simplest answer to these questions is that it's just the way God chose to do it! But I think a closer look is warranted. It's about *shared selflessness*.

The dream was powerful. Dreams are like cinema—like a movie. There is a storyteller—or Scriptwriter. Characters—and actors to play their parts. And a set of scenes—the background upon which the story is told. Dreams offer much more detail than do words displayed in print.

8 | NO ORDINARY CAT

God chooses to communicate to us in dreams rather than through other means, at times, to achieve a greater impact—through the use of a variety of media, all at once, played out on the human projection screen of perception.[15]

And the fortune cookie? That was but a piece of the Script, Distributed by The Divine Cinematographer into space-time.

As to when written messages acquire meaning, I imagine some messages are predestined for only a specific individual or group. Others, perhaps, have multiple destinations, acquiring unique meaning for each new recipient.

But why a dream *and* a written message? Symbolism.

I received the dream, but Aaron received the fortune cookie. We shared parts of the message *like* we shared our love for Clawdia.

When Aaron first met Clawdia at my South Philly rowhouse she warmed up to him quickly—much quicker than to me! No more than five minutes after he laid on my couch to relax after his trip from D.C. did she jump into my bay window and peer down at him from the couch top. And seconds later she laid on his stomach, purring!

And when my parents visited, Clawdia joined my father on the pull-out sofa overnight. He told me the next day he heard claws on the mattress in the middle of the night. He then realized Clawdia wanted a nighttime snuggle buddy. When I arose in the morning to hear this story, Clawdia sat peacefully on the couch between my parents, eating cheese and crackers.

It was a shared relationship. Shared love. For once in her life Clawdia had a loving family. We made the end of her life meaningful. She left this world feeling loved and accepted.

It makes sense that The Divine Cinematographer and Scriptwriter distributed the message and meaning of Clawdia's journey among us.

God disbursed the message among us to emphasize what was most important: we gave Clawdia the loving family she desperately needed. Together, we loved her. Together, we shared *one of the most important things* we'd do.

An individual's selflessness is special, but a family's selflessness and acceptance is insurmountably special—the most profound statement of love. An example of what Christ did for humanity.

> For it was always in his perfect plan to adopt us as his delightful children, through our union with Jesus, the Anointed One, so that his tremendous love that cascades over us would glorify his grace—for the same love he has for his Beloved One, Jesus, he has for us. And this unfolding plan brings him great pleasure!
>
> —EPHESIANS 1:5-6 TPT[16]

And what about the fortune cookie that read, **"There is no such thing as an ordinary cat"**?

No cat—or any other living being, for that matter—is ordinary because each has special meaning to God and to his or her family through the bond of love. All living beings have value and come into our lives for a reason.

For Clawdia, the "special" meaning was about acceptance into the loving family she lacked—and deserved.

From my human viewpoint, I valued the same. And the lessons. The importance of attuning to the transitory, and the importance of selflessness—both individual and communal.

And of course, the joy of companionship cannot be overlooked. Clawdia increasingly trusted me and eventually let me pet her belly!

A Grand Summary

As we cultivate moment by moment living and hearts responsive to the Spirit, we can release our prejudgments. We can learn to appreciate the transitory, the oneiric aspect of our lives. For in each moment, The Divine Cinematographer creatively reveals the Script.

Anytime we act selflessly, whether individually or communally, it's *always the most important thing* we'll do.

Remember that selfless acts are often spontaneous and shared.

And that we are all special and deserving of selfless love.

There is no such thing as an ordinary cat!

Dream on!

PART TWO | THE ANGELIC

9. THE LENS

Angels come to help and guide us in as many guises as there are people who need their assistance. Sometimes we see their ethereal, heavenly shadow, bright with light and radiance. Sometimes we only feel their nearness or hear their whisper. And sometimes they look no different from ourselves...

—Eileen Elias Freeman [1]

AFTER BREAKFAST, **I** relaxed on a bench in the courtyard next to Baker Commons to clear my head and digest my meal. In ten minutes, I'd make the mile walk to West Campus for my morning class. But momentarily, the leafy branches above shielded the hot morning sun, refreshing me ahead of the long walk.

• • •

It was September 1991 and my first semester at Ohio State University. Over eighty percent larger than Rensselaer, the campus required significant acclimation.

Then, we relied on paper maps. We didn't have mobile phones and GPS to guide us. If you got lost, you just figured it out without technology.

The idea of transferring to Ohio State came at the suggestion of my cousin, John. His father—my uncle—passed and we talked by telephone. During one of our conversations, John excitedly suggested the opportunity.

Aaron and I both transferred to Ohio State. And though we weren't clear yet what we would study instead of architecture, we saw an opportunity to explore academically and get to know our cousins.

• • •

I jerked my head upward. I almost fell asleep on the bench. But I needed to get going.

I arose for the long walk.

I paused, already a quarter of the way to class. I reached in my right pocket. The monocular lens I used to see better in class was missing.

Already, I passed Hale Hall, the South Oval, and Mirror Lake. And as I stood on the south lawn of Thompson Library, I pondered whether to return to the bench.

I prayed. I couldn't afford a new one.

God, please help me find it!

9 | THE LENS

You know that with my eyesight I need it and rely on it!
Please send an angel to guard it!
Send a female angel with blonde hair. And have her say, about the lens, "I was going to take it in somewhere, but I decided not to." That way, I'll know she's an angel sent to guard it.
I expect and trust that you'll keep it safe until I find it!

I pivoted and paced back across the lawn, past Mirror Lake, the South Oval, and Hale Hall. And across to the street to the courtyard.

I'm going to be so late!

I approached Baker Hall, scanning the area for the specific bench. It now had an occupant.

A pretty blonde woman my age graced the length of the bench. In her hands, she held an open book, but I didn't see its title. She donned a white shirt, peach-colored shorts, and new white running shoes.

How could a person be so pristine and clean!?

"Hello!"

No response.

"Um, hi! I'm wondering if you might've seen a small telescopic lens. I was sitting here about fifteen minutes ago and that was the last time I saw it."

She glanced up from her book and smiled.

"Yep. It's right here."

"Where?"

"There." She pointed at the bench.

The lens rested next to her in the crevice between two slats.

"Oh! That's it!" I said, relieved.

"I was going to take it in somewhere, but I decided not to."

My eyes and mouth widened. I stepped back and scanned the entire scene. Humbled and delighted, I beamed from ear to ear.

Oh. She's an angel!

"Well, thank you very much!"

"Sure!"

I wanted to stay. To talk with her. To see what would happen. But I knew I needed to get to class. After all, what would she say if I skipped!?

"I need to run to class. I'm going to be late."

No response from my angel.

I turned, preparing to leave, but then I looked back.

"So, you were guarding it!?"

She chuckled and responded with a drawn-out ***"Yessss!"***

Her inflection rose as she said it, as if she asked a question to match mine. A seeming combination of humor and sarcasm. After all, there was little uncertainty about this meeting!

These angels have a sense of humor!

I walked briskly to class but then slowed my pace.

If God sends angels when I need them, I certainly can trust him when I'm running late!

Finally, I made it to West Campus and the refreshing air conditioning of Kottman Hall.

I entered the lecture hall and eyed an empty seat next to Aaron. We both took Natural Resources Survey together.

I walked quietly down the carpeted steps to the empty chair, sat, leaned over to Aaron, and whispered.

"I have an interesting story to tell you."

"Oh?" he whispered back.

"Yeah. I'll tell you later."

9 | THE LENS

"Where were you!? He already took attendance!"

"Okay. I'll tell you later."

I sank into the seat and swung its tablet in place.

Flop! I dropped my spiral notebook on the desk in front of me. The sound garnered a glance from the professor.

I sat, poised, with pen in hand. But I couldn't concentrate. I was too focused on what I just witnessed.

Sight

FOR THE SKEPTIC what I witnessed might seem like coincidence. But, as Eileen Freeman reminded us in the epigraph to this chapter, angels sometimes look just like us.[2]

The angel images we're accustomed to seeing in books and art lead us to believe that's how angels look. Baby cherub angel figurines. Paintings of angels dressed in white, adorned with wings and glowing halos. But is that how angels look?

First, let's look at what we know about angels.

According to the Bible, angels are spirit beings, there are various ranks of angels in heaven, and they can appear in multiple forms.[3]

There are at least four types of Godly angels. There may be more. The Bible mentions the following four types.

Cherubim[4] guarded the entrance to the Garden of Eden[5] and accompanied the Ark of the Covenant and God's glory in the temple.[6] The Bible states God is enthroned above, between, or among the cherubim,[7] and rides upon them.[8]

Seraphim surround God's throne and worship him continually,[9] as do the *living creatures* who look like a lion, an ox, a man, and an eagle.[10]

Archangel means *chief messenger*, and though the Bible identifies Michael as—possibly—the only archangel, Daniel 10:13 describes him as "one of the chief princes" (NIV).[11]

But what do angels look like?

Following, are descriptions from King Daniel, Isaiah the Prophet, King David, and Jesus.

King Daniel encountered angels at least twice. The first encounter is found in Daniel chapters 3 and 6. The second, in chapter 10, follows. What a beautiful description!

> . . . behold, there was a certain man dressed in linen, whose loins were girded with [a belt of] pure gold of Uphaz. His body also was like beryl [with a golden luster], his face had the appearance of lightning, his eyes were like flaming torches, his arms and his feet like the gleam of burnished bronze, and the sound of his words was like the noise of a multitude [of people or the roaring of the sea].
>
> —DANIEL 10:5-6 *Amplified Bible* (AMP)[12]

Though you're likely familiar with many of the elements Daniel described, you might not be familiar with one of them.

Beryl, a gemstone, occurs in a variety colors. *Emerald* (green), *aquamarine* (blue), *morganite* (pink), *goshenite* (clear like diamond), *bixbite* (red), and *heliodor* (shimmering gold).[13]

9 | THE LENS

Imagine a being whom you could only describe as dressed in linen with a body of shimmering gold beryl; with a face like lightning and eyes like fire; a belt of gold and feet of gleaming bronze; a voice like a multitude or the roaring sea!

It's easy to read powerful scripture passages such as this and quickly move on from them. Imagine what Daniel felt. He must have been mesmerized by this sight!

But other encounters reveal different images. Isaiah saw a vision of angels—the seraphim—standing above Jesus.

> Standing above him were the angels of flaming fire, each with six wings: with two wings they covered their faces *in reverence*, with two wings they covered their feet, and with two wings they flew.
>
> —ISAIAH 6:1-2 TPT[14]

And some accounts depict angels carrying swords.

> So he drove out the man; and he placed cherubim at the east of the garden of Eden, and a flaming sword . . . to guard the way to the tree of life.
>
> —GENESIS 3:24 WEB

> David lifted up his eyes, and saw Yahweh's angel standing between earth and the sky, having a drawn sword in his hand stretched out over Jerusalem.
>
> Then David and the elders, clothed in sackcloth, fell on their faces.
>
> —1 CHRONICLES 21:16

> David built an altar . . . and called on Yahweh; and he answered him from the sky by fire on the altar of burnt offering.
> Then Yahweh commanded the angel, and he put his sword back into its sheath.
>
> —1 CHRONICLES 21:26-27

And what about the function or purpose of angels?

Angels bring messages from God, provide protection, help those who are hurt or who need strength, punish sin and bring judgment, and praise and worship God.[15]

King David wrote the following words emphasizing angelic protection is available to all who revere God.

> The angel of the Lord stooped down to listen as I prayed, encircling me, empowering me, and showing me how to escape. He will do this for everyone who fears God.
>
> —PSALM 34:7 TPT[16]

Before Jesus's crucifixion, an angel strengthened him as he prayed in the Garden of Gethsemane.

> "Father, if you are willing, remove this cup from me. Nevertheless, not my will, but yours, be done." An angel from heaven appeared . . . strengthening him.
>
> —LUKE 22:41-43 WEB

And, according to Jesus, children have angels too!

9 | THE LENS

> See that you don't despise one of these little ones, for I tell you that in heaven their angels always see the face of my Father who is in heaven.
>
> —MATTHEW 18:10

St. Paul reminds us that some people we meet are angels!

> And show hospitality to strangers, for they may be angels from God showing up as your guests. Identify with those who are in prison as though you were there suffering with them, and those who are mistreated as if you could feel their pain.
>
> —HEBREWS 13:1-3 TPT[17]

My encounter with the angel on the bench was my first. There were many others after, and you'll read about them in the following chapters. But it didn't take multiple meetings with angels to learn some things. It's hard *not* to come away from such an experience changed in some fashion.

First, I learned *God hears and responds to prayer.* Especially faith-filled prayer. I earnestly prayed to recover the lens. And I expected an answer. I expected God would send an angel. (Though, I was *still* surprised when I returned to the bench!)

Jesus made it clear that when we ask God for something, believing we'll receive it, that we *will* receive it. He said, "I am telling you, whatever things you ask for in prayer [in accordance with God's will], believe [with confident trust] that you have received them, and they will be given to you" (Mark 11:24 AMP).[18]

There are, however, some other conditions to receiving from God beyond praying with faith: the *in accordance with God's will* part.

Deliberate disobedience to God's commandments can certainly keep us from receiving.[19] Confession (of sin) is the only path to God's forgiveness and grace. Forgiveness is essential!

John the Evangelist said, "But if we freely admit our sins *when his light uncovers them*, he will be faithful to forgive us every time. God is just to forgive us our sins *because of Christ*, and he will continue to cleanse us from all unrighteousness" (1 John 1:9 TPT).[20]

Cultivating a forgiving heart is essential to receiving from God. Jesus said, "Whenever you stand praying, forgive, if you have anything against anyone; so that your Father, who is in heaven, may also forgive you your transgressions" (Mark 11:25 WEB).

And dwelling on our past failures—so that they define us and look bigger than God's promises—can extinguish faith,[21] as can an attitude of pride—that we know better than God.[22]

The second point of learning is that *angels have a sense of humor*. When I asked my angel whether she guarded the lens, she chuckled. You'll also read about a humorous angelic encounter in chapter 13. In my experience, God and the angels do have a sense of humor. I encourage you to look for such examples in your own life!

Thirdly, I learned *God deeply cares about every detail of our lives*. And in this case, the detail was my eyesight.

Having low vision isn't easy. And helpful technology, such as a monocular lens with a magnification power of eight and a twenty-one-millimeter objective lens, is expensive. Losing such items makes life frustrating and difficult.

I believe God answered my prayer, not only because I prayed with faith, but because he genuinely cared about me and my situation.

God cares deeply about us and all the details of our lives. This is evident by the words Jesus spoke to a large crowd.

> What is the value of your soul to God? Could your worth be defined by an amount of money? God doesn't abandon or forget even the small sparrow he has made. How then could he forget or abandon you? What about the seemingly minor issues of your life? Do they matter to God? Of course they do! So you never need to worry, for you are more valuable to God than anything else in this world.
>
> —LUKE 12:6-7 TPT[23]

I found more that day than just an item essential for seeing physically. God gave me spiritual sight. When the angel spoke the words I asked to hear as a confirmation, my faith grew!

As you read on, remember the following words from Psalms. "For he will put his angels in charge of you, to guard you in all your ways." (Psalm 91:11 WEB).

10. AMTRAK ANGEL

For You have been a strong-place for those who could not help themselves and for those in need because of much trouble. You have been a safe place from the storm and a shadow from the heat. For the breath of the one who shows no pity is like a storm against a wall.

—Isaiah the Prophet [1]

SPRING OF 1996. A trip to Connecticut. My first long distance trip alone. I hadn't thought much about it. I just believed everything would work out. Therefore, I did little planning, and I hadn't considered that might lead to a problem. After all, I was young, inexperienced, and feeling adventurous.

A year prior, in the summer of 1995, I sought counseling from an Idaho-based healing ministry. I recently finished a book by the ministry's founders, and I believed in their mission and method.

So, I called and spoke with a woman who referred me to a counselor in Virginia.

"You'll have to write her. She doesn't have a phone. Would you be interested in connecting with her?"

"Possibly. But I live New York."

"Well, I understand. However, you could write her and see what she says. She may know of some other counselors who aren't on our list. Some of them have their own separate ministries now. The ministry has grown a lot."

"Oh. Well, okay."

"Hold on. I'll get her information."

Virginia. That's probably not going to work.

"Okay, do you have a pen handy?"

"Yes."

I scribbled the address on a pad.

"Thank you!"

"You're welcome! I wish you the best on your journey!"

I sent a note. Later that summer, I received an envelope with a response. A recommendation to contact a ministry in Newtown, Connecticut. Closer to me, but not much.

I made a call. And it turned into several phone counseling sessions with Glenn.

Then, I learned the ministry planned a training retreat. It would take place in a year at My Father's House, a Catholic retreat center in Moodus, Connecticut. I had a year to plan.

• • •

10 | AMTRAK ANGEL

I sat on the floor by gate seven, my back against a support column. I just finished the six-hour trip from Syracuse to Penn Station in Manhattan. And it would be another two hours before my departure to Connecticut.

And I sat there until my departure time, anxious about what to expect next—a much different approach than I take nowadays. I've learned to relax and explore.

• • •

Though that was my first time traveling through Penn Station, I visited New York City twice prior—as a teenager, and again in 1994 with my brother and friends.

I remember well, the trip with my family as a teenager. We visited the Statue of Liberty, the Empire State Building, and the Word Trade Center. And I vividly recall the fast-descending elevators of the original World Trade Center. Fast enough to feel weightless—a little air space beneath my feet. As I stood in the descending elevator, The Inner Voice spoke.

Don't ever come back here! These towers may fall someday!

The message made me feel uneasy.

Perhaps something like that could happen. But, then again, no. Could a structure like this fall? Nah. Probably not.

The uneasiness lingered until the excitement of the city once again consumed me. And I forgot about it—until some years after the collapse of the towers, when I shared the memory with Aaron. I learned God spoke the same to him in the elevator.

Many years later, in 1998, I awoke from a dream trembling and afraid. In the dream, I stood in an elevator of a tall skyscraper. But I felt the urge to vacate it. And as I exited, others entered. The scene changed. I sat in a large lecture-style meeting room filled with people. Suddenly, I heard a loud rumble. I looked above me. The elevator I exited crashed through the ceiling. And the dream abruptly ended.

I prayed about the dream and its meaning. I even shared it with others. But I didn't understand it until several years later.

Both the internal nudge and the dream were prophetic messages. Oh, how I pray that we will not only hear from God, but also understand and act on what he speaks to us!

Part of me feels guilt when reflecting on these memories. *Could I have asked more fervently for understanding? Was there something I could have done to warn people?*

But I'm human. And I've grown spiritually since. And perhaps not all messages require a subsequent action.

But regardless, reflecting on these moments—and the disaster that occurred seven years later on September 11, 2001—motivates me to pray for understanding and for how to respond when I hear from God prophetically.

• • •

"Now receiving passengers at track eleven east for Northeast Regional number ninety-four, scheduled to depart at five thirty-eight."

"Track eleven east, now boarding for New Rochelle, Stamford, Bridgeport, New Haven, Old Saybrook, New London, Mystic, Westerly, Kingston, Providence, Back Bay, and Boston. Eleven east."

I grabbed my bag and walked quickly across the Penn Station concourse to gate eleven. A long line already formed at the gate.

10 | AMTRAK ANGEL

It would be two and a half more hours until my final stop—Old Saybrook, Connecticut.

Eight o'clock. My final stop.

I grabbed my bag and exited the train.

As I approached the red clapboard and white-trimmed depot, constructed in 1873 and now a historic landmark,[2] an aroma as ancient as the structure itself wafted from its interior. Woody, musty, and sweet. A perfume of old, from the post-Civil War era. A Reconstructionist masterpiece.

The depot's interior looked original. The walls were drab white; the windows and doors were trimmed in dull gray. Old, schoolhouse stem-mount pendant lights hung from the ceiling in an orthogonal pattern.

I walked to the ticket counter.

"Hello! Do you have a payphone?"

"You need to make a phone call?" said a man from inside the office. He bent forward to see me through the left window.

"Yes, I do," I said.

"Well, I don't got a pay phone. But I might let you use my phone back in here!"

In front of him at the window sat a young woman with long, straight, red-brown hair. Plainly dressed, with a large wooden cross around her neck.

"I really like your necklace!" I said.

"Thank you!"

She looked straight at me, into me, or through me. She'd been quiet until now. And I wondered about her—why she sat at the window so quietly.

"Who do you need to call? I'll dial the number for ya," said the station manager, now standing next to the young woman.

He called and handed me the phone.

"Hi. Glenn? This is Jason. I'm here."

"Jason. Oh, yes. Jason. You're where?"

"I'm at the train station. In Old Saybrook."

"Oh! Well, we're not expecting anyone until tomorrow. How can I help you?"

"Oh. I just assumed there were arrangements for when I got here."

"Hold on, Jason." He put the phoner aside to speak with his wife. "Jason? We haven't ever had a situation like this before. Do you have a place to stay?"

"Um. No. That's what I was calling about."

"Well, are you able to find a hotel for the night?"

"Oh! I see. I thought My Father's House would have accommodations."

"Well, they will, but not until tomorrow night. And we don't usually take people here at our home for the conferences. We're in Newtown."

"Oh, I'm sorry! I assumed you, or somebody, would meet me. Or that My Father's House would be available."

"See if you can get a hotel. But, if you have a problem, please give us a call back?"

"Okay. I'll try to get a hotel."

"Okay, Jason. We look forward to meeting you tomorrow."

"Thank you!"

"Goodnight."

I suddenly realized my error. I traveled all the way to Connecticut, assuming Glenn, or someone from his ministry

10 | AMTRAK ANGEL

would meet me at the train station. Or that the retreat center would accommodate me. I felt embarrassed and anxious.

"So, no!? They wouldn't take ya!?" said the manager.

"No. They said, 'Find a hotel.'"

"Oh, man! What kind of organization is this?"

"It's a Christian ministry. They're good."

"What!? Not if they can't give you a place to stay! Hah-hah! You sure it ain't a cult!?"

"No! It's not."

"Mmm. I dunno man!"

He and the young woman laughed—at me and with me.

Then, the young woman spoke.

"No! This one is okay. He'll be okay."

How would she know?

My curiosity piqued.

"So, I need to find a hotel."

"No, man! I'm gonna find you a hotel."

"That would be really nice of you."

"Come back in here!" he said, opening the office door.

After flipping through the telephone directory he made calls to several hotels.

"Oh, man! Mm-mm! Everything booked!"

"Huh! I wonder why?" I said, now quite nervous.

"Mmm. Everybody hookin' up 'n' doin' their thing, that's what! Mm-hm!"

The young woman smiled but said nothing.

I turned to her. "So, yeah. I like your Cross! Are you a Christian? I am!"

"You could say that!" she said, tilting her head.

"Any particular denomination?"

"No. I guess I'm a little bit of everything!"

"Oh. That's nice! How long have you been a Christian?"

"I guess I kind of always have been!"

"Oh, okay! So, you work here too?"

"Nope!"

"Oh!"

Now I was really curious.

With a tone of surprise and shock, the station manager said, "No! She don't work here! She doin' the same thing you are!"

"Oh! So, you're traveling too!"

She was silent.

"You might say that! She travelin' all over da place!"

I scanned the floor for her luggage.

"Oh, so that's your stuff!" I pointed to items on the office floor that looked like luggage.

"Nope."

I looked again. I now saw an old wooden chest with books stacked on it. My brain hurt. My mind played a trick on me. There wasn't any luggage.

She's an angel!

"Okay, man. I found you a hotel. But it's almost an hour from here! There ain't nothin' else! Nothin'! Everyone booked!"

"Where is it?" I said.

"North of New Haven!"

"New Haven! Isn't that back a whole train stop?"

"Yep. It sure is!"

"Well, I guess I'm gonna need a cab."

"Yeah, you certainly will! But I'll call for you. And let you talk to 'em."

10 | AMTRAK ANGEL

I held the phone to my ear waiting for a dispatcher.

"Taxi!" a gruff female voice rasped.

"Hi, I need a cab from Old Saybrook Amtrak station."

"Where ya goin'!?"

"I'm going to the Hilton Garden Inn, at 1181 Barnes Road, in Wallingford."

"For you!?" Who the hell do you think you are!?"

"I'm simply calling for a cab, ma'am."

"I'm not doing anything for you! You're a loser."

"Excuse me!?"

"You heard me!"

My heart raced.

"What are you talking about? I'm just calling for a cab. I don't even know you!"

"I don't care! I'm not helping you!"

"Are you serious? I don't understand."

"I'm serious."

"Well, that's really disrespectful. I can't believe what I'm hearing right now."

I hung up.

"I can't believe the way this dispatcher just treated me!"

I continued to recount the distressing conversation to the manager and young woman.

"That ain't acceptable man. I'm calling her back!" said the manager. "We use them all the time! I ain't never sendin' her our customers again!"

He called.

"The way you treated my customer is unacceptable! I will never, ever send our customers to you again. Ever! Do you understand me? This is an innocent man here!"

He hung up. The word *innocent* grabbed my attention.

How would he know whether or not I'm innocent?

I now wondered about his conversations with the young woman prior to my arrival. Had the young woman's presence and words influenced him? Perhaps even prior to my arrival?

"I'm gonna get another cab for you. But I gotta start closin' up first."

Closing up!?

I panicked. The manager then shut the gate over the window and walked out of the office, leaving me with the quiet, young woman.

"Come out here!" she said, walking to the waiting room.

I followed her and peered out a window onto a corner of the platform.

"Well. We could sleep outside tonight!" I joked.

"Hah-hah! Both of us?"

"Yup!"

"That might be a bit rough!"

"Yeah. I guess you're right!"

I walked to a bench and sat.

"I'll be back in a few minutes."

She turned and walked away.

Jesus, I am so hungry! I really need food!

The young woman immediately spun around and paced quickly back to me.

"Are you hungry?"

"Very!"

"I'm really not supposed to do this, but come back here," she said, opening the office door.

She can hear my silent prayers!? She's definitely an angel!

10 | AMTRAK ANGEL

"There's pizza here. Have as much as you'd like."

A found the box on the counter and took a slice. Then another. It was cold but yummy.

"I'll be right back!"

After several minutes, she and the manager returned.

"Okay, we gotta get you a cab," said the manager. "I'll call for you."

"Hopefully, this one will be better," I said.

"He should be fine with this one," said the young woman.

How would she know?

Ten minutes passed. The cab arrived. The driver came into the station to find me.

"Hey, Jason?"

"I'm Jason!"

"Hi Jason! I'm Brad. You ready to go?"

"Yup!"

"Follow me!"

I turned to thank the manager and the young woman. But only he remained.

Where is she?

"Hey, thanks for all your help!"

"That's alright! You have a safe night, okay!?"

"Please tell the girl who was here I said thanks!"

"Um, I will if I can find her!" he said.

"Are you friends?"

"I never seen her before in my life. Not until you came!"

⦿⦿

"Okay, we've got to go to through New Haven," said Brad.

I proceeded to the car's right, rear door.

"Hey, you can sit in the front!"

"Oh, okay!"

"We can talk. It's an hour trip. Depending on traffic."

We conversed at a gridlocked intersection.

"So, this is New Haven. Have you ever been to New Haven?" said Brad.

"I've been to Yale, once. But not around in the city."

"Well, it's an interesting place."

"So, are you from here?" I said.

"Yep. I am. Where are you from?"

"New York. Syracuse."

"What brings you to Connecticut?"

"I'm going to a week-long conference at a Christian retreat center in Moodus."

"Oh! Moodus! When are you going there?"

"Tomorrow morning."

"Just so you know, that's like another hour trip."

"That's alright. Thanks for letting me know!"

"So, I'm Catholic. I've had something on my mind. Do you mind if I ask you a question?"

"No! What is it?" I said.

"Do you think hell exists?"

"Hmm. That's an interesting question."

"I mean, I believe heaven exists. But…"

"Yeah. I think so. I believe there is a hell."

"Wow. Because I've really been struggling with that. I've had a lot of questions on my mind lately about all that stuff."

"I understand! I'll pray for you about this."

Dusk turned to night, and after eleven hours of travel—and unexpected events—I looked forward to a soft bed.

10 | AMTRAK ANGEL

"It's right up here on the left," said Brad. "I gotta get over in the other lane."

He pulled up to the hotel.

"Hey, do you mind if I pray for you?" I said.

"Sure! That would be nice. You have a nice night!"

"Um. I was gonna pray for you now."

"Wow! No one has ever offered to pray for me like that!"

"Well, I want to."

We prayed.

Shelter

AMONG ALL THE things that can happen in a day—and in life, for that matter—I ended up in the office of an old train station in Connecticut with a station manager and an angel. Then, in a cab with a driver who needed spiritual direction and strength. All because I failed to plan. Like I said, I was young, adventurous, and inexperienced.

I wonder what would've happened if the young woman weren't present.

Would the manager have refused use of the phone? I only had enough change for one phone call, and mobile phones weren't a thing then.

Would I have eaten any food that night? I hadn't eaten since early morning.

Would I have secured a cab ride and a hotel? The hotels were booked; the initial dispatcher was cruel.

I would have spent the night without shelter in an old town I didn't know. But an angel appeared.

I faced a lot of interference en route to the week-long retreat. But the kingdom of God manifested in my difficult circumstances. God ensured I arrived safely. And the week turned out to be life-changing.

The Mystery of the Kingdom

The Bible characterizes the kingdom of God as mysterious. I suspect that's because it's not readily visible to us, and because it's characterized in several contrasting ways.

First, the kingdom is characterized as *shelter*. The Psalmist wrote, "He who dwells in the secret place of the Most High will rest in the shadow of the Almighty" (Psalm 91:1 WEB), and "He will cover you with his feathers. Under his wings you will take refuge. His faithfulness is your shield and rampart" (Psalm 91:4).

And Jesus said, "The Kingdom of Heaven is like a grain of mustard seed which a man took, and sowed in his field, which indeed is smaller than all seeds. But when it is grown, it is greater than the herbs and becomes a tree, so that the birds of the air come and lodge in its branches" (Matthew 13:31-32).

The kingdom of God is also *within* and *among* us. We can see this in the following conversation between Jesus and the Pharisees, the strictest Jewish sect of the day.[3]

Notice the *Amplified Bible* Classic Edition (AMPC) emphasizes *in* and *among*.

> Asked by the Pharisees when the kingdom of God would come, He replied to them by saying, The

10 | AMTRAK ANGEL

> kingdom of God does not come with signs to be observed *or* with visible display,
>
> Nor will people say, Look! Here [it is]! or, See, [it is] there! For behold, the kingdom of God is within you [in your hearts] *and* among you [surrounding you].
>
> —LUKE 17:20-21 AMPC[4]

And although the kingdom of God has *already come*, it is also *yet to come*.

Theologian George Eldon Ladd (1911-1982) wrote eloquently about this.

> While the resurrection of the dead remains an event at the last day, in the resurrection of Christ this . . . event has already begun to be unfolded. The "halfway" point is passed. The early church found itself living in a tension between realization and expectation—between "already" and "not yet." The age of fulfillment has come; the day of consummation stands yet in the future.[5]

The kingdom of God also comes *wherever the Spirit of God manifests* and in *acts of healing.*

Jesus said, "But if I by the Spirit of God cast out demons, then God's Kingdom has come upon you" (Matthew 12:28 WEB).

He also said, "Heal the sick . . . and tell them, 'God's Kingdom has come near to you'" (Luke 10:9).

And, lastly, *where angels are present*, the kingdom of God is manifest, as evidenced by the following words Jesus spoke to Nathaniel.

> I assure you and most solemnly say to you, you will see heaven opened and the angels of God ascending and descending on the Son of Man [the bridge between heaven and earth].
>
> —JOHN 1:51 AMP[6]

So, in summary, the kingdom of God is *shelter*. It's *within* and *among* us; here *now* and *yet to come*. And *manifest in the presence of the Spirit, healing, and angels.*

Mercy and Grace: Eleos and Charis

In Old Saybrook, the kingdom of God manifested through an angel—to establish communication, offer comfort and sustenance, protect me from the wrath of the angry dispatcher, arrange transportation, and secure shelter.

God cares about every aspect of our lives, providing help even when we err. I was young and inexperienced; I failed to plan. But God showed mercy (*eleos*—withholding of punishment), and grace (*charis*—unmerited favor).[7]

The epigraph for the current chapter, from Isaiah, captures the overall meaning of meeting my Amtrak Angel.

> For You have been a strong-place for those who could not help themselves and for those in need because of much trouble. You have been a safe place from the storm and a shadow from the heat. For the breath of the one who shows no pity is like a storm against a wall.
>
> —ISAIAH 25:4 *New Life Version* (NLV)[8]

11. INFORMATION PLEASE!

Then Elijah lay down under the bush and went to sleep. An angel came to him and touched him. The angel said, "Get up and eat!" Elijah looked around, and by his head there was a cake that had been baked over coals and a jar of water.

—Jeremiah the Prophet [1]

I OFTEN SAY that my years working in food service and grocery taught me as much about people as my degrees in counseling and social work! I learned patience—first and foremost, and I learned the value of service, respect, and kindness. I also learned to bring joy into my conversations with customers. And these habits spread to my life outside of work.

During those years, 1998-2003, and in that environment, I experienced several angelic encounters. You'll read about them in the current and subsequent two chapters.

My angelic visitors came with important messages. Some presented human personality characteristics that tested my patience, kindness, and joy. And one angel visited a coworker after my brother and I prayed.

I call this period in my life The Grocery Years. I learned a lot then—and that there are more important questions than "Paper or plastic?"!

Peter's Groceries, a private grocery chain that operated in Syracuse, New York from 1944 to 2004 was unique. It had a small-town vibe the Peter family maintained throughout its lifespan. Basic décor. White floors, walls, and ceiling. Only a touch of color here and there. But in 2004, after sixty years, the competition from the largest companies like Price Chopper and Wegmans forced its closure.

It's in this environment—and during this time in my life—I grew tremendously, spiritually. Then, I attended a spiritually-alive church that unfortunately eroded into a cult-like mess.

I saw an excellent therapist. I learned what I didn't want—to continue working in grocery and food service. And I learned what I did want.

I became a rehabilitation counselor. Then a social worker. Then a life coach. A perfumer. And an author!

11 | INFORMATION PLEASE!

For a long time, breakfast frustrated me. I grew up eating cereal and orange juice in the morning. But I grew tired of that, after which I never settled on a consistent routine. What could I eat in the morning that is simple and easy to make? I had a talk with God.

I need help. Can you show me what to eat in the morning? What's a good breakfast option? I'm frustrated! I need information. Information please!

I forgot about my prayer.

Weeks later I stood at the front of aisle five, the frozen food aisle, stocking the first door on the left. That's where the huge bags of vegetables lurked. The ginormous bags seemed a lonely affair by themselves. Especially when there were options with which to pair them—like the Howard Johnson's macaroni and cheese all the customers coveted. (Sorry! It's no longer available.)[2]

Suddenly, I heard a voice from the back end of the frozen foods aisle

"Hello!"

I tuned toward the voice.

"Hello!"

A woman quickly paced down the aisle in my direction.

"Information please!"

Oh, no. Darn customers!

"Information please!"

She kept coming, and soon she stood next to me.

"How can I help you?" I said.

She was short. Probably in her sixties. Curly gray hair.

"Well? Have you ever considered waffles for breakfast!?"

"Um. I've had waffles for breakfast. Yes. Why?"
"With yogurt and fruit on top!?"
"No, I haven't, actually."
"Well, you should try it! It's really good. You just take a frozen waffle and put it in the toaster. Then you put some plain yogurt on the top and some fresh fruit! It's really good!"

She peered up at me through her silver glasses with curiosity. And I glanced down the aisle toward the waffles.

"What kind of waffles? Which brand?"
"Well? Any brand! It doesn't matter."
Wait. She's not here to get information for herself.
My curiosity piqued as it does in these situations.
"Okay! I will try it! Thanks so much for the information!"
She's an angel!
I looked at her. *You're an angel*, I said in my head.
"Well, okay then! I need to get going!"
"Is there anything else you need?"
"No. You have a nice day!"

She rounded the front of aisle five and proceeded to six.
I'm gonna catch her!

I prided myself on having grown smarter about these encounters—so I thought.

I hurried after her to aisle six. She was gone! Vanished. I checked aisle seven. Nope! Searched up and down the front. She was nowhere to be found!

Impossible! I was only a second behind her.
They sure are sneaky!
In the future I will catch them!

11 | INFORMATION PLEASE!

Sustenance

THE EPIGRAPH FOR this chapter is from a section of 1 Kings that describes a showdown between Elijah the Prophet and God, and King Ahab and the prophets of Baal and Asherah.[3]

The year was 863 BC.[4] The place: Mount Caramel.[5]

The worship of false gods was increasingly a problem for the Israelites, and Elijah sought to address it.[6] He called all the Israelites and the prophets of Baal and Asherah to join him and Ahab on Mount Caramel.

They prepared two bulls for sacrifice: one for God and the other for Baal and Asherah. Elijah and the prophets each called on their god to consume their sacrifice with fire. Whichever god responded would be revealed as true.[7]

The prophets called on Baal and Asherah all morning to no avail, but Elijah, after thoroughly dousing his sacrificial bull with water, prayed, and God consumed it with fire.[8] Then, Elijah annihilated all the false prophets.[9]

Defeated, Ahab returned home to his wife Jezebel to tell her the news.[10] (Ahab and his wife were the most wicked leaders Israel had known. They oversaw 850 prophets; 450 who worshipped Baal and 400 who worshipped Asherah. And they killed many true prophets of God).[11]

When Jezebel learned what Elijah did, she threatened his life.[12] Elijah, the strong, courageous prophet and warrior, now petrified with fear, fled a day's trip into the desert.[13]

Finally, Elijah took shelter under a juniper tree. And before sleeping, he asked God to take his life. He thought he failed. Though he served God faithfully, the Israelites wouldn't hear him. They continued to worship false gods, they killed God's prophets, and now Jezebel wanted to kill him.[14]

But an angel appeared to Elijah. And not just any angel. The angel of the Lord! Jeremiah the Prophet wrote about it.

> Then Elijah lay down under the bush and went to sleep. An angel came to him and touched him. The angel said, "Get up and eat!" Elijah looked around, and by his head there was a cake that had been baked over coals and a jar of water. He ate and drank and then went back to sleep.
>
> Later the Lord's angel came to him again, touched him, and said, "Get up and eat! If you don't, you will not be strong enough to make the long trip." So Elijah got up. He ate and drank and felt strong. Then Elijah walked for 40 days and nights to Mount Horeb, the mountain of God. There Elijah went into a cave and spent the night.
>
> —1 KINGS 19:5-9a ERV[15]

God wasn't finished with Elijah. Not at all. In fact, a long journey awaited him. And God saw to it he had the sustenance and strength required for his journey.

In Every Detail

My situation may seem unimportant compared to Elijah's, but both scenarios show God's concern for our adequate sustenance and strength. My journey doesn't need to look like

11 | INFORMATION PLEASE!

Elijah's to matter to God. And your journey, though it may appear different than mine, matters no less. God cares about every detail of our wellbeing. Even when we've failed—or think we've failed!

In Ordinary and Extraordinary

Sometimes the veil between heaven and earth parts, revealing God in extraordinary ways. But the rest of the time, we must learn to see God in the ordinary aspects of our lives.

James Henry Ecob (1844-1921), a minister in the Presbyterian, Congregational, and Unitarian churches, who spent much of his life in the areas I've lived—Albany and Buffalo, New York; Philadelphia, Pennsylvania—said the following about seeing God in the ordinary.

> If we can hear the voice of God in all sounds, see the sweep of His will in all motions, catch hints of His taste in all beauty, follow the reach of His imagination in all heights and distances, and trace the delicate ministry of His love in all the little graces and utilities that spring and blossom about us as thick as the grass, we shall tread God's world with reverent feet as if it were a temple. The pure and solemn eyes of the indwelling soul wilt look forth upon us from every thing which His hands have made. Nature will be to us, not some dark tissue of cloth of mystery flowing from some unseen loom, but a vesture of light in which God has enrobed Himself; and with worshipful fingers we shall rejoice to touch even the hem of His garment.[16]

Our challenge is to stay alert, believing God will meet us—rather than reverting to the mechanical, mindless ways of living that dull our hearts. When we do, we'll see God everywhere!

But whether we encounter God in the ordinary or the extraordinary, we *can* trust He always watches us and provides the sustenance and strength we need for our journeys.

The Veil Removed

And the veil we perceive between heaven and earth? It's thinner than we think. And in a real sense it doesn't exist! Jesus destroyed the veil through his death and resurrection, giving us direct access to God through him. God showed this symbolically by tearing the temple curtain that separated the people from The Holy Place and The Holy of Holies.[17]

According to scholars, the temple veil was thirty feet in length and sixty feet in height. And although no one knows for certain its thickness, some references state it was a handbreadth—up to four inches thick! We do know, however, that the veil was at least thick enough to obscure the view of the contents it shielded.[18]

Can you imagine witnessing the tear? Its appearance and sound? It was a *big* rip! The Gospel of Matthew describes it.

> Behold, the veil of the temple was torn in two from the top to the bottom. The earth quaked and the rocks were split. The tombs were opened, and many bodies of the saints who had fallen asleep were raised; and coming out of the tombs after his resurrection, they entered into the holy city and appeared to many.

11 | INFORMATION PLEASE!

> Now the centurion and those who were with him watching Jesus, when they saw the earthquake and the things that were done, were terrified, saying, "Truly this was the Son of God!"
>
> —MATTHEW 27:51–54 WEB

And here are some contemporary depictions, through film, of the veil removed—a short film and a true story.

First, I highly recommend *The Veil Removed* (2019), directed by Branden J. Stanley.[19] It is an absolutely beautiful film regardless of whether or not you are Catholic.

Secondly, I recommend *Thanksgiving Blessing*, from season 2, episode 10, of *It's a Miracle* (1999).[20] It's a powerful, moving story, highlighting the meaning I've conveyed in this chapter.

In Receiving and Giving

In chapter 10 you read how an angel helped me secure shelter, transportation—and pizza. Now, in chapter 11, you've read about water and bread—and waffles with yogurt and fruit!

You might conclude God likes pizza and waffles. I won't dissuade you if that's the conclusion you've made!

But why *wouldn't* God care about our basic needs? He created the metabolic process that sustains life and the fuel it requires.

But you might ask, "What about homeless people? Starving people? Those without clothes or shelter?" Hear Jesus's words. God tasks *us* with helping those who suffer.

> He also said to the one who had invited him, "When you make a dinner or a supper, don't

call your friends, nor your brothers, nor your kinsmen, nor rich neighbors, or perhaps they might also return the favor, and pay you back. But when you make a feast, ask the poor, the maimed, the lame, or the blind; and you will be blessed, because they don't have the resources to repay you. For you will be repaid in the resurrection of the righteous."

—LUKE 14:12-14

In Summary

As you read on, remember God is intimately involved in your daily life despite the salience of your activities. He's in *every detail* of your life. In the ordinary *and* extraordinary. He cares for you when you're faithful *and* when you fail, during your times of contentment *and* times of suffering, when you're satiated *and* when you're famished. He's in receiving *and* giving. And He'll give you *all* the strength and sustenance you'll ever need.

The veil is removed! You can enter The Holy of Holies!

So, journey on!

You never know what you'll discover.

Or whom you'll meet!

12. SILENCE!

An untrustworthy messenger stirs up trouble, but a faithful emissary is curative balm.

—King Solomon [1]

THE GROCERY STORE was mostly a peaceful place to work. And I met many kinds of people there. Most were friendly, but some people—customers and coworkers—were disrespectful and challenged my patience.

There were also funny encounters. I recall the evening a man with a thick mid-eastern accent approached me in the pet food aisle. He asked, "Where are da un dom?"

I asked him to repeat it twice because I had difficulty understanding him. The third time he nearly shouted, "Cohn. Dumbs!" I barely contained my laughter as I informed him the condoms were up front, behind the service desk.

Realizing he'd have to ask once more for "un dom," at the service desk, he replied with a whimper, "Oaaakay!" and turned to make his way to the front.

But not all encounters were humorous.

One afternoon, as I knelt beside a bottom shelf in the pet food aisle stocking cat food, Damon, a new worker, approached me and started a conversation.

"Hey! You want a crystal?" he said.

"For what? What would I do with it?"

"You swallow it, man!"

"Why?"

"It gives you crazy energy and power!"

"Uh, no thanks!"

"I just want to help everyone I can, man! I'm a witch!"

"I'm all for helping people. I just can't do that though. I'm a Christian."

After that exchange, Damon annoyed me with rude or vulgar comments. One time as I bagged a customer's groceries, he waltzed in from outdoors, happy to share his conversation with the septic serviceman.

"Hey! Did you see they're cleaning the septic tank?"

"I know. I saw."

"I just asked the guy if I could lick the stick!"

12 | SILENCE!

"That's gross. Why would you say that?"

"I've done it before!" he said, without shame. "It's not as bad as you might think!"

"Are you serious?"

"Yeah, I'm serious. I've done it several times!"

"You've eaten human feces."

"Several times."

"Damon, this is gross. I don't want to talk about this anymore."

I ignored him and continued bagging the customer's groceries.

After leaving the church that turned cult-like, Aaron and I looked for new churches to attend. Brandon from Produce invited us to his church.

I worked the Friday before we were to attend, and on my break, I encountered Damon in the men's room. I simply offered a friendly hello. His reply was not so friendly.

"Don't talk to me while I'm going to the bathroom!" he shouted.

"It doesn't matter," I said, nonchalantly.

"Yes it does!!!"

As he walked toward me, I thought he might try to pin me to the wall.

He continued screaming.

"Have a nice time at church this weekend!!"

How would he know I'm going to church this weekend?

I knew then it wasn't Damon who spoke, but a demon.

He stormed out of the restroom, slamming the solid metal door with a force I've seldom witnessed.

I stood motionless for a moment, my heart pounding. But then I heard God speak to my heart.

Don't be afraid. That's how much Satan hates when believers assemble together.

The Voice of Truth.

I inhaled and exhaled deeply and relaxed my body.

Wow! His reactions were completely out of proportion for the situation! That was definitely evil working through him.

God, I'm not afraid of him. I know what we're dealing with here. Please protect Aaron and me.

Despite Damon's attitude, I attempted to share Christ with him. I bought him a book. A story about a woman's salvation and deliverance from witchcraft. He read it in one evening.

The day after I gave it to him, I saw him in the parking lot on my way into work.

"I read that book!"

He didn't sound too enthused.

"Already!? What did you think?" I said.

"It was terrible All negative! Witchcraft isn't just about demons and stuff."

"Well, didn't you see any positives? There was a lot of that in there too!"

"I guess," he said. "But witchcraft isn't all dark. It's both dark and light."

I walked into the store and punched the timeclock to begin my shift, disappointed in his reaction.

12 | SILENCE!

One afternoon at home, Aaron and I prayed about the situation with Damon. We'd had enough.

"Let's pray God will silence him!" I said.

"Okay! Let's pray! It's really needed at this point."

We prayed together that God would silence Damon and quell the chaos he brought.

Some weeks later I again encountered Damon in the parking lot.

He bolted from the store in a panic.

"I don't know what just happened! "I don't know what just happened!" he said.

"What's wrong!?" I said.

"I just saw an angel!"

"Really!? What did the angel look like?"

"He was very tall! And bright! Glowing white!"

"Did he say anything?"

"Yes!"

"Well, what did he say!?"

"He just said, '**Silence!**' And he was serious!"

Though I knew what the angel meant, I asked Damon what he thought.

"Well, what do you think he meant!?"

"I, I don't know! All I know is I *must* do what he said!"

After that, Damon was silent for a long time. The encounter had quite an impact on him!

To be fair, Damon had a caring side. He could be kind and he was a good worker. He was even kind to me at times. But, invariably, he'd say or do something to screw it up for himself.

He acted out with Aaron too. But the incidents were not isolated to me and Aaron. He argued with the store managers too. I recall one particular incident Aaron witnessed that turned out to be Damon's last—at least for a while.

Aaron explained to me he prayed God would remove Damon from the work environment because he continued to cause problems. Then, several weeks later, he witnessed Damon arguing with the head manager.

The exchange led to Damon's termination.

But the way it happened was funny.

Aaron recalled, "I was up front, and Damon was standing there talking to Scott. Scott was behind the service desk. And Damon yelled to him, 'Thanks for firing me, Scott!'"

"Wow! Continue!"

"And Scott said, 'I didn't fire you!'"

"And?"

"And Damon yelled, 'Yes you did!'"

"What did Scott say?"

"He was just there laughing behind the desk! And Damon walked out. He just quit! I could barely contain my laughter!"

"He fired himself!"

"He fired himself!" said Aaron. "Isn't that crazy?"

"Yeah! It sure is!"

"I think what really happened, is God fired him!"

"I agree!" I said. "Sounds like answered prayer to me!"

"Definitely!"

"Hey! There's nothing like peace and quiet!"

God sent an angel to establish peace. It's amazing how different an environment feels when peace reigns.

12 | SILENCE!

In his absence there were no more disparaging or grotesque comments. No more arguments with management. Just silence and peace.

Peace

PEACE IS NOT always about silence. Sometimes it's about speaking out—about injustice or to offer comforting words. But, regardless, peace is clearly *never* characterized by chaos, confusion, and clamor. In the situation with Damon, however, silence *was* necessary in order to bring peace.

A Curative Balm

King Solomon wrote, "An untrustworthy messenger stirs up trouble, but a faithful emissary is curative balm" (Proverbs 13:17 *The Voice* [VOICE]).[2]

Unfortunately, Damon wasn't much of a trustworthy messenger or curative balm. But he could have been. I pray for him, that he will know the peace of God.

We have choices each day to either act as trustworthy messengers, faithful emissaries, and a curative balm for those we meet. Or to act as sources of heartache and discord.

Living as a peacemaker is a blessed life. Jesus said, "Blessed are the peacemakers, for they shall be called children of God" (Matthew 5:9 WEB).

And look how the *Amplified Bible* states the same verse. "Blessed [spiritually calm with life-joy in God's favor] are the makers *and* maintainers of peace, for they will [express His character and] be called the sons of God" (Matthew 5:9 AMP).³

Power, Love, and Wise Discretion

When we pursue God with our whole hearts, we can expect our faithfulness will be challenged. At times we'll want to cower with fear in the face of rejection, ridicule, or persecution. But God gives us the power to overcome.

At the end of his life, from prison, Paul the Apostle admonished his favorite mentee and friend, Timothy, saying, "For God has not given us a spirit of cowardice, but of power, and of love, and of wise discretion" (2 Tim. 1:7 *Darby Bible* [DBY]).⁴

In place of the word *discretion*, the *World English Bible* (WEB) uses the word *self-control*. The *King James Bible* uses the words *sound mind*.

In instances where we're threatened and desire to cower in fear, we must remember we have access to the Spirit who gives us power and love. And wise discretion, self-control, and a sound mind.

Damon (and the demonic presence in him) threatened me, and I almost gave into the fear I felt. But God reminded me of the truth. And I chose to think on—and take into my heart—the truth and the Spirit.

This is not just an intellectual assent, although it often begins there. When we meditate on the truth and allow the Spirit in our hearts, our character changes.

12 | SILENCE!

But we're not perfect by any means. There have been times I've given into fear. Some of these experiences were quite severe. You'll read about one of them in chapter 16.

But, after falling, I got back up, got help, recovered, learned, and moved forward. And that's what's important!

The writer of Proverbs 24 (possibly Solomon, but the actual author is unknown), said the righteous may fall seven times, but they get up each time. But the wicked? Not so much.

> Listen up, you wicked, irreverent ones—don't harass the lovers of God and don't invade their resting place. For the lovers of God may suffer adversity and stumble seven times, but they will continue to rise over and over again. But the unrighteous are brought down by just one calamity *and will never be able to rise again.*
>
> —PROVERBS 24:15-16 TPT[5]

Where Are the Peacemakers?

Peacemakers are difficult to find in the world today. But they're present—in the midst of the chaos. You may not notice them at first. They're ordinary people. They don't boast. But if you stick around long enough, you'll recognize them.

My mother is a peacemaker. I recall many times over the years where she brought peace and happiness among people at odds—whether at home, as a teacher, at church, or elsewhere.

My maternal grandmother was a peacemaker. She exuded love and a desire for everyone to be happy. I recall seeing her angry only once.

My father is a peacemaker in a different way than my mother. I've often heard him advocate for fairness. And it makes sense. Research shows when people use the word *fair* in negotiations they trigger a need to drop what's unfair.[6]

Leo, a former manager at Peter's Groceries where I worked, is a peacemaker. He had a way about him. Kind and caring. A strong Catholic man who radiated God's grace. He led by example, demonstrating unselfish servanthood. And it was contagious—at least for me. He was slow to judge, if at all, and willing to give anyone a chance. Today he is a high school history teacher. I imagine he has ample opportunity for peacemaking in that context!

And I think of the many counselors who guided me through the most difficult life storms. They certainly are peacemakers. Counseling is heavenly work. The Bible says, "Where no wise guidance is, the people fall, but in the multitude of counselors there is safety" (Proverbs 11:14 AMPC).[7] And also, "Carry one another's burdens and in this way you will fulfill the requirements of the law of Christ [that is, the law of Christian love]" (Galatians 6:2 AMP).[8]

Becoming a Peacemaker

But how does one become a peacemaker, not just in thought but also in deed?

First, we learn peace (or strife) from our family, friends, teachers, ministers, and other sources.

Regarding generation sin in families, the Bible states, "As for those who are not loyal to Me, their children will endure the consequences of their sins for three or four generations" (Exodus 20:5 VOICE).[9]

12 | SILENCE!

Spiritual blessing also passes across generations. There are statements about this throughout the Bible. Here are two examples from the book of Isaiah.

> I will pour refreshing water on the thirsty and streams on the dry ground. I will pour out my Spirit on your children, my blessing upon your descendants.
>
> —ISAIAH 44:3 TPT[10]

> "And this is my covenant promise with them," says Lord Yahweh. "From now on, my Holy Spirit will *rest on them* and not depart from them, and my *prophetic* words will fill their mouths and will not depart from them, nor from their children, nor from their descendants, from now on and forever," says Lord Yahweh.
>
> —ISAIAH 59:21[11]

In addition to receiving peace through our families and role models, we can pursue a relationship with God directly, allowing God to fill us with his grace and love.

When we're filled with the Holy Spirit, we naturally desire to bless others and bring peace. But to whatever degree we lack the Spirit in our hearts, we'll argue and sow discord.

Jesus is the ultimate peacemaker. It's His Spirit we need within us. When Jesus returned to his hometown, Nazareth, he stood in the synagogue and read the following words: Isaiah's prophecy about himself as the ultimate peacemaker.

> The Spirit of the Lord is on me, because he has anointed me to preach good news to the poor. He

> has sent me to heal the broken hearted, to proclaim release to the captives, recovering of sight to the blind, to deliver those who are crushed, and to proclaim the acceptable year of the Lord.
>
> —LUKE 4:18-19 WEB

So, to be peacemakers, we must know peace ourselves. We need examples of what peace looks and feels like.

Traumatized people often lack examples of peace. And some who have experienced trauma from an early age have never known peace. We're bound to relive and pass trauma to future generations until the cycle is broken.

We must take responsibility for the pain of our past. No one else will do it for us. Of course, we don't have to do it alone. We are participants with God in this process. And seeking the help of others is crucial.

Peacemakers are tasked with caring for the brokenhearted; for being a curative balm. Here are some examples from Scripture.

King Solomon wrote, "Do not withhold good from those to whom it is due, when it is in your power to act" (Proverbs 3:27 NIV).[12]

And Apostle Paul wrote, "*So now what?* We who are strong are not just to satisfy our own desires. We are called to carry the weaknesses of those who are not strong" (Romans 15:1 VOICE).[13]

12 | SILENCE!

And there's many more examples! Proverbs 19:17 and 22:9. Isaiah 61:1-3. Matthew 5:16, 5:42, and 25:35-40. Luke 6:38, John 15:12, and Acts 20:35. Galatians 6:2, Philippians 2:4, Hebrews 13:16, James 2:14-17, and 1 John 3:17.

Angels as Peacemakers

As we participate with God in peacemaking, at home, at work, or in our communities, we'll sometimes come across situations that are difficult to handle. And some we find impossible to face on our own.

In such circumstances we need an intervention. God and His angels are just a prayer away.

Remember Jesus's words: ". . .if two of you on earth agree (harmonize together, make a symphony together) about whatever [anything and everything] they may ask, it will come to pass *and* be done for them by My Father in heaven (Matthew 18:19 AMPC).[14]

13. BUTTER ANGEL

And sometimes they look no different from ourselves—until, their work done, they leave suddenly, quietly, with only a hint of halo or a wisp of wing behind to make us wonder.

—Eileen Elias Freeman [1]

AFTER WORKING GROCERY and food service jobs for six years, I was seriously ready for something new. In fact, I was depressed. I had potential, but I felt stuck. It took me some time to figure out a new direction.

I was age thirty and earning just above minimum wage. Six years prior, I completed a bachelor of music, but I chose not to pursue an education degree. I wasn't interested in teaching music. And that left me with few job opportunities. So, I continued working in a grocery store until I had a plan.

There's nothing quite like stocking frozen foods in the winter in Central New York. I recall many days going into the store from severe winter weather, only to walk into the frozen foods freezer moments later.

And there were the times I managed the frozen department when the manager was on vacation—for no extra money. This included ordering stock. I recall the order coming in once and realizing I had four gigantic pallets of frozen food that reached above my head.

Of course, we all were a pretty good team. Two managers and some coworkers set the rollers end to end on milk crates, creating a conveyer, proceeding from the stock room into the freezer. We cleared all four pallets in no time.

When you're profusely sweating in a freezer while stocking frozen food items, you know you're probably working too hard for minimum wage!

After that, I learned to avoid mistakes, like over-ordering, that resulted in working harder than my measly pay called for. I'm a hard worker, and I'm okay with putting in extra time and effort when necessary. But there is *hard* work, and there is *smart* work!

Occasionally I also stocked the dairy department. That tended to be less stressful because dairy is kept at a higher temperature. Make no mistake. Cold is stressful!

13 | BUTTER ANGEL

One day, as I casually stocked the butter, I reached a point of depression that called for answers. I needed a plan to do something new, and soon! My joy faded, my attitude jaded, and my energy sapped, even just stocking butter felt like a chore.

I zoned-out as I repeatedly grabbed boxes of Land O' Lakes from the grocery cart next to me and placed them neatly in the cooler.

Someone grabbed my shoulder from behind and spoke simultaneously. His grip was firm and I smelled his cologne.

"You're blocking my butter!"

I turned to see a man with a bright countenance and a big smile. This was someone full of joy. His mood contrasted sharply with mine.

I tried to muster a smile through my depressed state, but it faded quickly.

The man laughed heartily, then repeated himself.

"You are blocking my butter!"

I felt jealous of his joy, but not ready to match his energy. And I sensed his disappointment.

I should just have fun. Be more lighthearted!

Rather than let his playfulness lift my spirit, I felt agitated and angry.

I need more butter.

I pushed my cart to the stock room and entered the dairy cooler to locate the remainder of the sale butter. It appeared the week's stock was dwindling. I grabbed what was left and returned to the aisle.

To my surprise, my friend, whose butter I blocked, stood in my place, silently watching the butter stock. In my spirit, I felt he prayed.

Is he praying? I wonder why he's still here?

The man didn't have any groceries in his arms nor did he have a cart. He wasn't shopping.

Suddenly, I knew. And I was determined not to let him get away!

I spoke to myself and to him, in my head.

He's an angel!

You're an angel!

He turned and looked directly at me. Then he bolted!

He ran as fast as he could through aisle six, past the diapers to the right and the beauty items to the left!

With nothing in his hands, and no shoulder bag, and no grocery cart, he was quick. He whizzed to the front and I was determined to catch him.

I was right behind him, but I wasn't fast enough.

Where'd he go!?

He vanished.

I quickly scanned the cash registers, the left front door and the right front door. Afterward, I checked every aisle. But he was nowhere.

I stopped, out of breath.

Why would he run like an athlete—in a grocery store?

The words he spoke echoed in my head.

You're blocking my butter.

But he didn't even get any butter!

Suddenly I was aware of my mental state and attitude.

He was full of joy. And I couldn't even receive it. I really was blocking his butter. Maybe not physical butter, but butter, nonetheless.

I thought about the meaning of the encounter for many days and weeks.

13 | BUTTER ANGEL

He came not to receive, but to give me something. Just like my angel who recommended waffles with yogurt and fruit.

There was a message. And I needed to pay attention. To understand.

Joy

WHAT IS THE significance of butter? When you think of butter, what comes to mind? What thoughts, feelings, and memories? I imagine you have no negative experiences with butter.

Butter is the secret ingredient. It's what makes good cookies. And what are pancakes and veggies without it? Butter is golden yellow like a morning sunrise.

And you may associate butter with breakfast on a sunny, Saturday morning, with holiday celebrations, or with other heartfelt gatherings of family and friends.

Butter and joy go together!

The bible has something to say about butter too—where Isaiah prophesied about Jesus's birth.

> Therefore the Lord Himself shall give you a sign: Behold, the young woman who is unmarried *and* a virgin shall conceive and bear a son, and shall call his name Immanuel [God with us].

> Butter *and* curds and wild honey shall he eat when he knows [enough] to refuse the evil and choose the good.
>
> —ISAIAH 7:14-15 AMPC[2]

What Isaiah meant is Jesus would discern right from wrong even as a baby—while still eating baby food.

According to research, toddlers begin discerning right from wrong at about nineteen months.[3] And babies can usually stop jar food and start eating soft, solid food at around twelve months.[4]

Isaiah is conveying here, that Jesus was *born* knowing right from wrong—a powerful statement about his virgin birth.

It's a beautiful detail, easily missed through quick reading. Here, there's an association of butter and the joy of Jesus's birth.

So, what did my visitor mean by **"*You're blocking my butter!*,"** a statement he repeated twice—with a sense of humor?

He wasn't there for butter. He didn't take any for himself. He came with an analogy. I blocked the physical butter (a symbol of happiness) like I let my attitude shut out the spiritual butter (joy).

It's okay to feel down. It's a natural part of our lives in this world. And some people struggle with melancholy more than others. But there is a way out!

When Jesus spoke to his disciples about his pending death and resurrection, he said, "I have told you these things, so that in me you may have peace. In this world you will have

13 | BUTTER ANGEL

trouble. But take heart! I have overcome the world" (John 16:33 NIV).[5]

The Passion Translation is quite expressive with this verse!

> And everything I've taught you is so that the peace which is in me will be in you and will give you great confidence as you rest in me. For in this unbelieving world you will experience trouble and sorrows, but you must be courageous, for I have conquered the world!
>
> —JOHN 16:22 TPT[6]

So we *will* experience trouble and sorrow in this world. But when we let ourselves enter a cynical state where we blunt or block our reception of—or participation in—the joy that only comes from God, that's a concern. And that's where I was at when I blocked and stocked the butter.

The angel invited me to participate in joy, and at the time I wasn't open. I felt sad and guilty afterward. But I considered the message.

I needed to keep my attitude in-check so as to not block out joy. After all, for those who know God, joy is freely available! And the more love we receive and give, the brighter we shine!

I absolutely love the following verse. It's one of my favorite passages in *The Passion Translation*. It's about shining brighter. You'll smile as you read it! I know I do!

> But the lovers of God walk on the highway of light, and their way shines brighter and brighter until they bring forth the perfect day.
>
> —PROVERBS 4:18 TPT

This joy is available to all who seek it. There's always a way out of despair! Even if it takes time and support!

Communion

I WAITED FOR the Drumlins bus at the corner of East Washington Street and South Warren Street. I was headed home. And I was still in that period of exploring what to do next in my life.

I'd like to say I fully learned the lesson about joy from my Butter Angel, but I still had work to do.

He came back.

I paced as I waited for the bus, making a game out of stepping on the cracks between the sidewalk tiles. So, I didn't notice him at first.

But out of the corner of my eye, I glimpsed someone mimicking my movements. He too appeared to pace, but he hummed joyfully.

How is he so joyful!?

I studied his behavior. Nothing bothered him, as if a holy flame within sustained him.

It was him! The Butter Angel!

"So, you want to know how it happened for me?"

He got down on his knees in a praying position.

"Ahh! I see," I said, not knowing what else to say.

He rose to his feet.

13 | BUTTER ANGEL

"And you need to find a good church! That's really important!"

That was true. I hadn't been back to church consistently since leaving the cult-like one. And he knew!

I felt vulnerable. I hadn't changed my attitude since I saw him last.

"Which church? Which do you recommend?"

"Any of them! There's a lot of good ones out there. They're all over the place!"

I felt like laughing, but I was embarrassed. I was immediately aware I let my feelings about one church generalize to all churches. I'd become cynical not only about my life stage but about churches too.

The bus rolled up. And I walked quickly to its door.

From the first step, I looked back at him.

"Any? Are you sure!?"

"Absolutely!"

I took a seat on the bus and that's the last I saw him.

As I gazed out the window, I pondered the meaning of his messages. About joy. About communion with God and others. And I thought about my attitude.

I have some work to do!

14. DRUNK IN THE PARK

When pride comes [boiling up with an arrogant attitude of self-importance], then come dishonor and shame, But with the humble [the teachable who have been chiseled by trial and who have learned to walk humbly with God] there is wisdom and soundness of mind.

—King Solomon [1]

OCCASIONALLY I WALED downtown from my house. An hour trip. I often walked through Syracuse University on the way, as I enjoyed staying connected to my alma mater—even if just to pass through the campus. The walk was good exercise but also gave me time to think. And then, I did a lot of thinking about my future—what I might do other than working in a grocery store.

There isn't much that's exciting in downtown Syracuse other than Armory Square. Usually I made these trips for an appointment or to take a bus elsewhere.

One particular summer afternoon stands out. I don't recall the reason for my trip downtown, but I do recall the incident that happened on my way there.

I walked through Syracuse University and downhill to East Genesee Street. Past Syracuse Stage toward the Interstate 81 bridge.

Just before the bridge, East Genesee Street splits, and in between is Forman Park. Just as I approached the old Parkview Hotel building on my right, I noticed a man sitting in the park across the street to my left. He sang loudly.

Oh, there's a drunk man, sitting in the park. Probably homeless. Who cares? I shouldn't be so judgmental!

As soon as I thought it, the man rose to his feet and crossed the street quickly. He headed toward me.

"It's a beautiful day! A beautiful day, isn't it?"

Though I still clung to my disappointment about my current situation, I agreed.

"Yes it sure is!" I said as confidently as I could.

Then he was on the sidewalk with me.

"You're right I'm a drunk man! I've been sitting in the park all morning! But at least I give my whole heart to God!"

"That's great!" I said. "I believe too!"

"At least I give my whole heart to God!"

He had my attention!

14 | DRUNK IN THE PARK

Here we go again! I know he's an angel!
"Hey, can I ask you a question?"
"You can ask me anything!"
He was pretty clairvoyant for a drunk man.
"Is there still time left? You know. Before the end?"
His countenance softened and a smile appeared.
"Yes, yes. There's still time. There's still time."
"Okay. That's good," I said. "Because sometimes I wonder."
"I'm going to pray for you. It won't take long."
I was quite surprised.

And I was in just the right spot, near a utility pole by the Parkview Hotel. He gently pinned my back to it.

Thoughts of my safety kicked in, but he wasn't finished. He placed his hand on the top of my head and began to pray.

"Dear Heavenly Father, bless this man. Draw him closer to you! Show him your heart and the purpose for his life!"

Then he switched from English to a foreign tongue.

One minute I was walking downtown and now I'm pinned against a pole by a man I don't know and he's praying for me with his hand on my head!

I briefly questioned how I get myself in such situations, but I dismissed the thought.

The man finished his prayer.
"In the mighty name of Jesus, Amen!"
"Thank you! I really appreciate that."
"You're welcome! And you have a nice day."
"Yes. You too!"
I turned to leave.
"And don't worry about anything!"
"Thank you!"

On the remainder of my walk to downtown, I thought about the man's words: ***"You're right I'm a drunk man!"*** and ***"At least I give my whole heart to God!"***

Though I didn't consider myself a judgmental persons, I knew I was prone to it at times, like most people. And I drank occasionally. I didn't have an issue with it, and I didn't mind if others drank. But I found myself judging the guy in the park.

But I left with a clear message about humility.

Humility

PREVIOUSLY YOU READ, in chapter 6, that believing in—and obedience to—God requires overcoming pride. Humility is the opposite of pride. But what is it and why is it important? How do we humble ourselves and what are the consequences if we don't? How does pride impede our connection to God and how can humility help? And what does this have to do with meeting an angel in Forman Park?

Humility Defined

Most non-religious definitions of the word *humble* include terms such as *insignificance, subservience, inferior, low importance,* and *low quality*.[2]

The religious meaning of *humility*, however, isn't suffering and humiliation, but acknowledging self and others for exactly who God created them to be—not more or less. Humility is *appreciation*—not *depreciation*—of one's own *and* others' talents, skills, and virtues.[3]

Pride is thinking we're more or less than God created us to be—that we have a better idea about who we are and how to live than God does.

King Solomon warned about the consequences of pride. Here are his words.

> When you act with presumption, convinced that you're right, don't be surprised if you fall flat on your face! But walking in humility helps you to make wise decisions.
>
> —PROVERBS 11:2 TPT[4]

Other Bible versions use the words *shame* and *disgrace*. The *New International Version* states, "When pride comes, then comes disgrace, but with humility comes wisdom (Proverbs 11:2 NIV).[5] And, *The Voice* states, "When pride comes, shame is not far behind, but wisdom accompanies those who are humble" (Proverbs 11:2 VOICE).[6]

Pride leads to shame, disgrace, and falling flat on one's face! There's a rhyme for you to remember!

But why is humility important? Is it really necessary?

The Importance of Humility

King Solomon wrote, "Trust in the Lord with all your heart and lean not on your own understanding; in all your ways submit to him, and he will make your paths straight" (Proverbs

3:5-6 NIV).⁷ And Proverbs 22:4 states, "Humility is the fear of the LORD; its wages are riches and honor and life" (NIV).⁸

And look how the *Amplified Bible* expands the same verse. "The reward of humility [that is, having a realistic view of one's importance] and the [reverent, worshipful] fear of the LORD is riches, honor, and life (Proverbs 22:4 AMP).⁹

When we lean on our own understanding and fail to view ourselves realistically, we're acting as gods of our lives. We've hindered or blocked our connection to God. Through pride, we also hurt ourselves and others.

This is why humility is important!

In order to have faith we need humility. We must acknowledge we know little about this vast universe in which we live. We must cease acting as gods of our lives.

And to put it simply, *doubt* has its root in *pride*. When we doubt, we're basically saying we know better than God how all this works.

We elevate science, technology, fortune, and fame above God. We attempt to rid the world of the spiritual aspect of life because it doesn't fit our belief systems. Doubt and disbelief become a way of life. And it doesn't work!

That's why we're now seeing—in the western world especially—a shift (back) toward spirituality. Multitudes are in agony for lack of a hope that's bigger than themselves.

Humility requires we relinquish our judgmental attitudes. When we judge ourselves we're saying we're not that great and

14 | DRUNK IN THE PARK

God made junk. When we judge others we're saying the same about them. And none of it is true!

All humanity, the animals, and the world, were created by God—with love. So, when we choose to love instead of judge, we align ourselves with the nature of God's kingdom.

And what does the Bible say about God's kingdom? It's *within* and *among* us![10] Therefore, it's not the external appearance of right and wrong that matters. It's whether we love. Whether we allow God's kingdom to reign in and through our hearts, and in our communities.

The Pharisees and Sadducees, the strictest Jewish sects of Jesus's time on earth, failed to understand this. And Jesus let them know it. They were concerned with religious rules and the appearance of holiness rather than the state of their hearts.

On the Jewish Sabbath, as Jesus and his disciples walked through a wheat field, his disciples picked and ate the grain. Some Pharisees saw this and said, "Look! Your disciples shouldn't be harvesting grain on the Sabbath!" (Matthew 12:2b TPT).[11] And here is Jesus's response.

> Jesus responded, "Haven't you ever read what King David and his men did when they were hungry? They entered the house of God and ate the sacred bread of God's presence, violating the law by eating bread that only the priests were allowed to eat.
>
> And haven't you read in the Torah that the priests violated the rules of the Sabbath by carrying out their duties in the temple on a Saturday, and yet they are without blame? But I say to you, there is

one here who is even greater than the temple. If only you could learn the meaning of the words "I want compassion more than a sacrifice," you wouldn't be condemning my innocent disciples. For the Son of Man exercises his lordship over the Sabbath.

—MATTHEW 12:3-9 TPT[12]

Jesus warned us not to be like these people. He said, "For I tell you, unless your lives are more pure and full of integrity than the religious scholars and the Pharisees you will never experience the realm of heaven's kingdom" (Matthew 5:20 TPT).[13]

His point? We can't have a real, living relationship with God if we're consumed with religious rules and the external appearance of holiness, but haven't taken time to do the heart work necessary to know God.

And *that* requires humility!

My Forman Park angel warned me of the same by saying, **"You're right I'm a drunk man! But at least I give my whole heart to God!"**

That's pretty much the equivalent of Jesus rebuking the Pharisees for condemning the disciples as they ate grain on the Sabbath. His comment hit deep and I realized I had work to do at the heart level!

Ironically, several years later I interned at a rescue mission. I counseled people who became homeless and addicted to substances after years of trauma, and I met people with six-figure salaries who ended up in the same situation. The

14 | DRUNK IN THE PARK

homeless and addicts are just like you and me, needing love rather than judgment.

Resolving Doubt

One evening in 1991, while eating dinner with Aaron at Ohio State University, we saw a group of students from the fellowship we attended. Their conversation centered around a student who struggled significantly. We prayed for him.

The student struggled with doubt. I recall him saying, with his head in his hands, "I can't take one more doubt!" I felt for him. I too was familiar with doubt. There were times I doubted God or my standing with him. I think most believers experience doubt at some point.

Faith is not contingent on a perceptual experience of God. This simplest path from doubt to faith is believing without proof. Childlike faith. This is partly what Jesus meant when he said, "Truly I tell you, anyone who will not receive the kingdom of God like a little child will never enter it" (Matthew 18:3 NIV).[14]

I learned years later, however, that doubt is often not an intellectual matter. Resolving persistent doubt is not a matter of forcing oneself to believe more strongly. It's resolved through obeying God's voice. That's because faith and obedience are two sides of the same coin. They go together.

Of course, first one must hear. So, the person who persistently doubts should pray, "God, please speak to me. Let me *hear* your voice." And the second prayer should be, "God, please help me to *heed* your voice." As soon as we respond to God's lead, our doubt fades, because we've tapped into the Spirit's living guidance. This is what Jesus meant when he said,

"My sheep *respond as they* hear My voice; I know them *intimately*, and they follow Me" (John 10:27 VOICE).[15]

Doubt can also be a sign a person needs a touch from God. Have you experienced Unexpected Grace? The Manifest Presence? Doubt disappears when we're filled with the Holy Spirit!

Faith without evidence, for sure, is precious. It always is! But we can also know God intimately. We can continually hear from him and respond to his direction. It's a relationship we grow into! Look what Paul wrote about this!

> This gospel unveils a continual revelation of God's righteousness—a perfect righteousness given to us when we believe. And it moves us from receiving life through faith, to the power of living by faith. This is what the Scripture means when it says: "We are right with God through life-giving faith!"
>
> —ROMANS 1:17 TPT[16]

Thomas, one of Jesus's disciples, struggled with doubt. Though he wasn't present when Jesus met his disciples after his resurrection, the other disciples told him later. And Thomas said, "Unless I see the nail marks in his hands and put my finger where the nails were, and put my hand into his side, I will not believe" (John 20:25b).[17]

A week later, all the disciples gathered in a house with the doors locked. And Jesus appeared out of nowhere. Poof! He either walked through a wall or appeared inside the dwelling from out of thin air!

This is an easy point to miss. Look at the following verse and you'll see it. "Then eight days later, Thomas and all the others were in the house together. And even though all the doors were locked, Jesus suddenly stood before them! 'Peace to you,' he said" (John 20:26 TPT).[18]

But Thomas *still* needed proof! Did Jesus scold him? Not at all. Notice Jesus's greeting of *peace*. That included Thomas!

And what was Jesus's response to Thomas? He helped him believe! Here is the conversation between Jesus and Thomas.

> Then, looking into Thomas' eyes, he said, "Put your finger here in the wounds of my hands. Here—put your hand into my wounded side and see for yourself. Thomas, don't give in to your doubts any longer, just believe!"
>
> Then the words spilled out of his heart—"You are my Lord, and you are my God!"
>
> —JOHN 20:27-28 TPT[19]

And then Jesus said, "Thomas, now that you've seen me, you believe. But there are those who have never seen me with their eyes but have believed in me with their hearts, and they will be blessed even more!" (John 20:29)[20]

Belief *without* proof is precious. Belief *after* proof is sometimes needed. And that's okay! If you need proof, ask! God is really good with helping people believe.

But why all this about *doubt*?

Because encountering angels—the topic of Part Two—is beyond many people's experience. And for some people—it's difficult to believe in a reality beyond their typical experience. Even if for just *one particular moment or situation.*

It's easier to say, "He's just a drunk homeless man in the park!" It's the easy way out. We don't have to move out of our comfort zones. We don't have to do or change *anything!*

There is a realm beyond our physical existence. But sadly, many people miss its wonder through persisting solely in material existence and their own limiting beliefs.

Ignorance is *not* bliss. It's misery. We can see this in all the destructive ways of living that exist in the world today—and that have existed since the beginning of time.

Without a belief in someone greater than ourselves, our hope dwindles and we self-destruct. But when we turn to God we find hope. And *that* is as simple as it can be said!

Summary

As you read on—and live on, I encourage you to relinquish your pride and doubt. Open your mind, heart, and spirit to the possibilities beyond yourself.

And always act with love. Because everyone needs it! And angels often appear and act in ways we don't expect!

Remember: "And show hospitality to strangers, for they may be angels from God . . ." (Hebrews 13:3).[21]

15. BIG MONEY

When fortune smiles and the stream of life flows in accordance with our wishes, let us diligently avoid all arrogance, haughtiness, and pride.

—Marcus Tullius Cicero [1]

SPRING 2007 WAS an important transition for me. I would soon graduate with a master's degree from Syracuse University, and I looked forward to landing a new job with a decent salary—especially because I had little cash and a big education loan. So, I prayed about the future. What job did God have for me? And where should I live?

As a counselor in training, I completed internships on the brain injury unit of a rehabilitation hospital, at a state psychiatric center, and at a rescue mission.

One morning, as I headed downtown for my internship at the rescue mission, I walked through the Hutching's Psychiatric center campus.

There were plenty of green spaces. I often found grassy, tree-covered spaces on my walk, which made it more enjoyable and peaceful.

There was one particularly pretty area I enjoyed. A grassy strip between Madison Street and Cedar Street, next to the old school that housed the Syracuse City School District offices. As I strolled through the spot, a man I'd never seen engaged me in a conversation.

He wasn't a psychiatric patient. He was dressed in a black suit and carried a leather shoulder bag. None of the psychiatric patients dressed like that. And he wasn't an employee there, as he didn't wear a state badge.

He was a tall African man. His attire, crisp and spotless.

"Good morning, sir! A beautiful morning isn't it?"

"Yes it is!"

"That's a nice shoulder bag you have there!"

"Oh, thanks! I've had this for a while. But I like it. It really has held out well. It does the job."

He was talking about the army green messenger bag I took everywhere. A Lucky Brand bag for men, no longer made. Extremely durable, cotton, with leather zippers, strap, handle. But my bag still wasn't as nice as his.

"Yours is really nice too!"

He held out his hand.

15 | BIG MONEY

"Nice to meet you Jason! My name is Big Money!"

"That's interesting! So, what's in the bag!?"

He said nothing.

I almost asked again, but suddenly realized that Big Money probably would have a bag full of cash!

"Okay Jason? So, just remember, my name is Big Money!"

He emphasized the word *big*.

"You'll be seeing more of me!"

We parted ways.

If he's not an angel then he's a psychiatric patient or drug dealer!

I laughed inwardly.

Nah. He's gotta be an angel!

I thought about the meeting and how I recently prayed for a decent-paying job.

God, if he's an angel, send him again!

And I kept thinking about his shoulder bag. It looked expensive. All black leather. Brand new!

What was in there that he was so silent about?

I began my job search. A substance use counselor position in Vienna, Virginia didn't work out. Public transportation, which I relied on, was sparse there.

But another opportunity emerged in Philadelphia. In December 2007 I accepted a job as a vocational rehabilitation counselor in Philly. And in January, I moved there.

But, meanwhile, I had an internship to complete and I still needed to graduate.

I caught the Drumlins bus from home and got off at Dunkin Donuts on the corner of South Crouse Avenue and Marshall Street. Grabbed a coffee and bacon, egg, and cheese bagel. Same pattern as many mornings that spring.

I again walked in the grassy space by the old school.

I wonder if I'll see Big Money again. God, please send him!

He didn't show, and I felt disappointed. But it was a beautiful morning. The grass was dewy, the sunrise pretty.

I thought about all my past accomplishments. Seven years of college to finally get a music degree. And four years of counseling school. I was excited for the future.

"Hey Jason! Here I am!"

I looked around but I didn't see him.

"Over here Jason! It's Big Money!"

"Oh, hi! Good to see you again!"

He waved to me from a distance.

"Have a nice day now!"

"You too!"

"Just remember! You'll be seeing more of me!"

Blessing and Abundance

CICERO ONCE SAID, "When fortune smiles and the stream of life flows in accordance with our wishes, let us diligently avoid all arrogance, haughtiness, and pride" (Cicero [44 BC] 1913).[2]

15 | BIG MONEY

If our response to blessing is pride and arrogance, we've missed the point. Pride sets us up for calamity. Remember? Pride leads to shame, disgrace, and falling flat on one's face!

A prideful response to blessing ignores others who suffer, who need their own blessings. The healthy response to blessing is gratefulness—with a desire to bless others.

Big Money came with an important message: I would see more of him. And he reminded me to not forget it! Had I responded without faith and with ungratefulness, I may never have seen the coming blessings.

But I expressed my thanks to God. And not long after, I started the highest paid job I ever held. And other blessings came my way in the years to come.

Blessing and Abundance

But what are blessing and abundance?

Blessings come in many forms. Here is Dictionary.com's definition of *blessing*.[3]

> 1. the act or words of a person who blesses
> 2. a special favor, mercy, or benefit
> 3. a favor or gift bestowed by God, thereby bringing happiness
> 4. the invoking of God's favor upon a person
> 5. praise; devotion; worship, especially grace said before a meal
> 6. approval or good wishes

And *abundance* is *a lot* of blessing! Here is Dictionary.com's definition of *abundance*.[4]

1. an extremely plentiful or oversufficient quantity or supply
2. overflowing fullness
3. affluence; wealth
4. *Physics, Chemistry.* the number of atoms of one isotope of an element divided by the total number of atoms in a mixture of the isotopes.

Ascribed Value

We ascribe value—to people, animals, things, places, and events—differently. Therefore, a blessing for one person may not seem like a blessing to another. What I see as abundance may not look like abundance to you.

But are we correct in the value we assign?

This is an interesting question to consider. You probably recall times when what you valued little ended up mattering a lot, and times when what you valued immensely turned out to have little significance.

The act of ascribing value is not as straightforward as it initially appears. There are entire fields of study dedicated to this topic: *value theory*[5] and *moral philosophy*.[6]

Intrinsic Value

Life stance[7] (the way of living based on what is deemed most important) determines an individual or group's *intrinsic values*[8] (which are desirable in and of themselves).

The *moral nihilism* life stance sees no right or wrong and therefore has no intrinsic value.

In *humanism* and *eudaemonism*, the intrinsic value is human flourishing; in *environmentalism*: life flourishing.

15 | BIG MONEY

In *feminism*, gender equality; in *multiculturalism*: acceptance and flourishing of values beyond one's group.

In *hedonism*: pleasure; in *utilitarianism*: utility, happiness, and pleasure.

In *rational deontologism*: virtue or duty; in *rational eudaemonism*: virtue and happiness; in *situational ethics*: love.

In *Judaism*: tikkun olam (desire to act constructively and beneficially); in *Buddhism*: enlightenment and nirvana.

And in *Christianity*: Imago Dei (created in God's image).

Inherent Worth

Do people, animals, things, places, and events have inherent worth? Most people believe humans[9] and animals[10] have inherent worth. But only Christianity views humans as created in God's image.

Genesis 1:27 reads, "So God created man in His own image, in the image and likeness of God He created him; male and female He created them (AMP).[11]

From a Christian view, this resolves every battle about worth. We are worthy because God created us in his image. Our value comes from beyond the veil—from God's kingdom.

And everything else flows from there—all blessing, abundance, and everything good. Jesus's brother, James, expressed this well. Here are his words.

> Every gift God freely gives us is good and perfect, streaming down from the Father of lights, who shines from the heavens with no hidden shadow or darkness and is never subject to change."
>
> —JAMES 1:17 TPT[12]

Don't Judge Your Blessing!

In chapter 8 you read about suspending judgment in order to engage with the transitory, fleeting moments of meaning and purpose. But it's not just these moments we miss through judgment. It's blessing and abundance too!

From the spiritual vantagepoint, blessing and abundance look quite different than from a nonspiritual view. From a kingdom view, blessing is about God's character. From a nonspiritual view, blessing is mostly about material goods.

If we subscribe only to the nonspiritual view of blessing and abundance, we'll end up living a life characterized by the temporal. But when we acknowledge blessing and abundance come from the kingdom of God, we get kingdom charter along with any blessing we receive—regardless of the kind of blessing.

And what is this character? All blessing and abundance from God carry *love energy*.

If we're to grow spiritually, we must make a shift. We must relinquish the temporal view of blessing and abundance and acknowledge the spiritual view. We must stop thinking in terms of giving and receiving material goods alone.

When we receive God's love, we resonate with *kingdom energy*. Our lives take on new form. Blessing becomes a way of life. And, sometimes, material blessings flow from it.

A Word of Wisdom

Some words of wisdom. Regarding blessing and abundance, remember the following: receive every blessing with a grateful heart, as many blessings are missed due to ungratefulness;

15 | BIG MONEY

blessings do not always appear as blessings; giving is the *modus operandi* for blessing and abundance.

You read about the first point earlier. The second and third points are important too.

First, we can sometimes overlook blessings that look like bad fortune. Blessings *can* be found in heartache and suffering. Or, if not in it, afterward.

When Jesus foretold his death and resurrection in the presence of his disciples, Peter rebuked him. Mark 8:22 (TPT) shows Jesus's response.

> . . . Jesus turned around, and glancing at all of the other disciples, he rebuked Peter, saying, "Get out of my sight, Satan! For your heart is not set on God's plan but man's!"[13]

I imagine Peter felt at least a bit insulted at Jesus calling him Satan. But Jesus wasn't speaking to Peter. He rebuked Satan who influenced Peter's words.

Jesus's death didn't look like a blessing at first. His disciples were emotionally devastated and wept.[14] But that wasn't the end. Jesus rose from death three days later.

After Jesus's resurrection, Mary Magdalene, Mary the mother of Jacob, and Salome entered the tomb together. This is what they found.

> But when they arrived, they discovered that the very large stone that had sealed the tomb was already rolled away! And as they stepped into the tomb, they saw a young man sitting on the right, dressed in a

> long white robe. The women were startled and amazed. But the angel said to them, "Don't be afraid. I know that you're here looking for Jesus of Nazareth, who was crucified. He isn't here—he has risen victoriously! Look! See the place where they laid him. Run and tell his disciples, even Peter, that he is risen. He has gone ahead of you into Galilee and you will see him there, just like he told you."
>
> —MARK 16:1-7 TPT[15]

Surely, not all blessings look like blessings. May we pray for discernment so that we do not respond like Peter did. For what we judge as lack, loss, sorrow, hardship, and death, may be the blessing and abundance we need! Proverbs 17:3 affirms this.

> In the same way that gold and silver are refined by fire, the Lord purifies your heart by the tests and trials of life.
>
> —PROVERBS 17:3[16]

Giving is the *modus operandi* for blessing and abundance.

Paul wrote to the Corinthians, "Remember this: Whoever sows sparingly will also reap sparingly, and whoever sows generously will also reap generously" (2 Corinthians 9:6 NIV).[17] And he also said, "Now he who supplies seed to the sower and bread for food will also supply and increase your store of seed and will enlarge the harvest of your righteousness" (2 Corinthians 9:10).[18]

15 | BIG MONEY

The giving principle is called the Law of Reciprocity, a concept that's had wide reception in the Christian community. For example, the American Episcopal clergyman and author Brooks Phillips preached about the Law of Reciprocity in the 1800's. See *Sermons Preached in English Churches*.[19]

The main principle of the Law of Reciprocity is that when we give, we lose nothing. We always gain in some fashion. We can see this in every aspect of life.

Tip a lit candle to light another, and the initial candle stays lit. You've doubled your light. In conversations, ask open-ended questions, listen carefully for people's responses, and thank them for their views and input. You'll receive the same kindness and understanding in return.[20]

And here is what Jesus said about giving!

> Give generously and generous gifts will be given back to you, shaken down to make room for more. Abundant gifts will pour out upon you with such an overflowing measure that it will run over the top! Your measurement of generosity becomes the measurement of your return.
>
> —LUKE 6:38[21]

Summary

Remember to open your heart. Love all people who cross your path. You may be their only source of help or encouragement. Or they may have blessings for you. And not everyone we meet is human. Some are angels!

And, when blessings come, be grateful. And remember Cicero's words. "When fortune smiles and the stream of life flows in accordance with our wishes, let us diligently avoid all arrogance, haughtiness, and pride" (Cicero [44 BC] 1913).[22]

And lastly, be generous. "Give, and it will be given to you. A good measure, pressed down, shaken together and running over, will be poured into your lap. For with the measure you use, it will be measured to you" (Luke 6:38 NIV).[23]

16. WHEN YOU FALL

The Eternal sustains all who stumble on their way. For those who are broken down, God is near. He raises them up in hope.

—King David [1]

I LEARNED THE hard way about burnout in July of 2011. At the time, I lived and worked in Philadelphia, Pennsylvania as a vocational rehabilitation counselor, and I just emerged from a week-long vacation in Cortland, New York—my childhood hometown—where the air smelled of fresh ozone, green grass, and summer woods. Much crisper and cleaner than the air in Philly.

Upon my return, and after exiting the 30th Street Amtrak station—as I walked south along 30th Street in the direction of Market Street and the Market-Frankford subway station to complete the remainder of my trip home—a huge windstorm kicked up endless shards and scrapings of Philly trash, shoving it in my face for several minutes.

It was a forceful attack! Looking back it seemed symbolic—like a foreshadowing of the life-storm that would soon darken my path. But that wasn't my first warning!

• • •

My commute from Oxford Circle in Northeast Philly to my job in Northern Liberties involved taking a bus and the Market-Frankford train.

Each weekday, I transferred between the bus and the train at Frankford Transportation Center. There was nothing desirable in Frankford, a run-down, crime-infested area that continually depreciated.

In 2015, Camille Moore, a freelance content writer for *Housely*, named Frankford one of Philly's fifteen toughest neighborhoods.[2] And Frankford also made *RoadSnacks* writer Sam Sparke's list of Philly's ten worst neighborhoods of 2020.[3]

On an evening in June, as I waited in the underpass by my bus stop, a man approached me. He was short with graying hair and reminded me of my Forman Park angel eight years prior.

He appeared to know exactly where he was headed, as he hurried over to me, anxious to talk.

"You know, going out to the bars to meet the ladies isn't what you think it is!"

16 | WHEN YOU FALL

"What do you mean?" I said, as I leaned on the brick wall beside me.

"People make a big deal about it, but it's not what you think it is. You never know where the girl you're talking to has been!"

"Yeah, I think I know what you mean."

I recently wondered whether going to the bars was a good option for meeting women. Though I'd visited bars before, I never considered them a decent place to meet a woman. But I questioned this. And the man spoke to my recent thoughts.

"No! I'm serious! Don't do it! You never know if the woman sitting by you was just with another man. Or maybe she just got a divorce! You don't know! I'm telling you!"

At this point I pushed myself off the wall and stood straight. He had my full attention.

He's an angel!

"I'm definitely listening. I hear what you're saying. I agree with you, that it could be a problem at times."

"There's plenty of other places you can go to meet people, you know. Church is a good place to meet a woman!"

"I hear what you're saying!"

He backed up and shuffled his feet.

"Oh! And do you know how to fall? You need to know how to fall!"

"What do you mean?"

"Well, here! Let me show you!"

I prepared for the demonstration.

The man swung his arms behind himself and bent them into L-shapes. He squatted on the ground and leaned back on his arms.

"Here! Like this!"

"Okay. I see!"

"When you fall, you wanna fall like this! With your arms out! You never want to fall on you back!"

"I see what you mean! So, giving yourself support."

"Yes! That's right!"

He stood and glared at me.

I felt uncomfortable, so I mustered a response.

"Umm. So. Okay. I want to get this straight. I'm taking everything you say to heart."

I spoke to myself and God.

He's an angel!

The man smirked.

"Yep!" he said and continued his gaze.

"Okay. So, don't waste time on frivolous relationships. Don't go to places where I'm not going to meet quality people. Women."

"Yep!"

"And when you fall, make sure you have support!"

"That's right!"

Apparently I heard the lesson correctly.

And just then, Bus 58 pulled in.

"Um. My bus is here. I gotta go," I said. "But thank you! I will think about everything you said!"

I stepped forward but he raised his hand.

"And one more thing!"

"Okay! What's that?"

"Read Psalms!"

I walked out from the underpass and he followed. And as I boarded the bus, I turned toward him.

16 | WHEN YOU FALL

Déjà vu.

I was in this situation before. I recalled standing on the first step of the bus in Syracuse eight years prior. At that time, I responded with anger when my Butter Angel challenged me to find a new church.

I was determined not to screw it up this time. I yelled over the other passengers who waited behind me.

"Which Psalm should I read!?"

"*Psalm . . .*"

I couldn't hear over the voices and the noise of the engine.

"What!!?"

"*Psalm . . .*"

Did he say sixty-four? Thirty-four? Thirty-seven?

"Okay!" I said.

"*It's really good! Read it!*"

I took note of his enthusiasm.

I felt joy about holding a Bible conversation among the bystanders. And it sounded like he enjoyed it too!

I sunk into a seat and thanked God for the meeting. And my mind wandered to the time I fell from a tree at age eleven.

• • •

It was autumn of 1983. The weather was still nice enough to wear shorts. Dad washed our Chevrolet station wagon in the back yard while I climbed the huge willow tree.

Should I stay on the thick branches or try the thin ones?

I felt like going out on a limb, so I stepped on the twigs next to me. But I underestimated their capacity to hold the weight of my eleven-year-old self.

The branch cracked under my feet.

I knew I would fall on my back, so I quickly placed my right hand behind my head to avoid a brain injury.

"Dad!!"

There was no time to say anything else.

I landed flat on my back with my hand still under my head. And there was only an inch between my hand and the ground.

I could've hit my head hard. And that would've been bad.

Dad looked and ran over to me.

I sat in the living room, recovering from the blow. I felt nausea and an impending sense of doom. I feared I might die.

Then I vomited several times.

But the school play was that night and I didn't want to miss it. I insisted I attend.

I vomited several more times during the play. Then, we made a trip to the hospital.

I recovered well. But to this day I have a slight bump on my right shoulder blade. Perhaps a bone fracture that healed improperly. I've never known for sure.

• • •

The weeks passed and July came. I escaped dirty Philadelphia and spent a one-week vacation with my family in New York. The air in Cortland was noticeably cleaner, and my break was peaceful and restful. But the week flew by. It was time to go back.

16 | WHEN YOU FALL

The wind blew dust and trash in my face for several minutes as I walked from 30th Street Station to the subway. The gust grew into a blast, forcing me to stop. I couldn't move. And this made me think.

Did I come back to a storm? God, please let it not be true!

The wind calmed and I continued to the subways station. But I had an uneasy feeling in my gut.

⁂

A week came and went. Things were great! It was a hot and humid day, very typical of the Philly summers. But the heat was especially unbearable that afternoon. Suddenly I found myself overwhelmed.

I was physically and emotionally exhausted. An unexplained sadness hung over me that I couldn't shake. My head felt foggy, and I couldn't focus on my work.

As I sat at my desk that afternoon, there were only a few coworkers present. I felt strangely alone as I experienced all these sensations. Finally, as I gave up and laid my head in my arms, I knew something wasn't right.

⁂

After a hospital visit and a follow-up doctor visit, I came face-to-face with the fact that what happened was stress-induced. Burnout! Multiple life and work stressors took their toll on me. And that was just the beginning.

Panic set in as I questioned my ability to cope. I took a medical leave but misunderstood the regulations. My paychecks stopped. And I was thrust into unstoppable panic. It quickly became the worst time of my life.

⁂

A year later, I resigned from my job in Philly. The uncertainty that followed was palpable. But, with time, therapy, medication, family, friends, and God, I made it through the storm and learned valuable lessons.

Hope

NOBODY IS IMMUNE from dark times and suffering. Not even the most sincere lovers of God. Jesus said in the world we will have difficulties. But he overcame the world.

> I have told you these things, so that in Me you may have [perfect] peace *and* confidence. In the world you have tribulation *and* trials *and* distress *and* frustration; but be of good cheer [take courage; be confident, certain, undaunted]! For I have overcome the world. [I have deprived it of power to harm you and have conquered it for you.]
>
> —JOHN 16:33 AMPC[4]

When we endure hardship we must remember there's no night without day. No night ever lasts so long that day won't come. And there's no storm that won't pass. For every storm there's tranquility that follows. And when we fall, we will rise.

King David wrote these encouraging words: "The Eternal sustains all who stumble on their way. For those who are broken down, God is near. He raises them up in hope" (John 16:33 VOICE).[5]

16 | WHEN YOU FALL

Even sincere followers of God in Biblical times suffered.

Joseph's brothers sold him into slavery, but when freed, he held a high position in government.[6]

Moses, chosen by God to lead the Israelites, grew so tired of their complaints, he asked God to kill him as a sign of compassion![7]

Naomi (which means *pleasant*) lost everything including her husband and sons. She insisted people call her Mara (which means *bitter*). But God restored her pleasantness and hope.[8]

Job lost everything! His wife told him to kill himself and his friends criticized him. But he remained faithful and God blessed the end of his life.[9]

Jeremiah constantly grieved because the Israelites refused to heed his prophetic warnings. Eventually the Babylonians captured the people. Jeremiah is known as the *weeping prophet*.[10]

Paul suffered much, including what he referred to as a *thorn in the flesh*. Though he prayed for its removal, God let it remain.[11] Even so, he stayed faithful to God.

King David, though highly prone to exceeding sorrow and great fear, served God faithfully.[12] And he wrote seventy-five of the 150 Psalms.[13]

A whale swallowed Jonah, but he miraculously survived.[14]

King Darius locked Daniel in a den with lions simply because of Daniel's righteousness. But God protected him. The lions did not harm him.[15]

Shadrach, Meshach, and Abednego refused to bow down and worship King Nebuchadnezzar, so he threw them in a blazing furnace. But God rescued them. They emerged unharmed.[16]

And many of the disciples, apostles, and prophets died gruesome deaths through crucifixion, beating, beheading, hanging, or other means.[17]

And let's remember Jesus's suffering.

He experienced grotesque torture! Yet, it's through his suffering we have the hope of eternal life.

Isaiah foretold, in detail, Jesus's crucifixion, years before it happened. Here are Isaiah's prophetic words.

> [For many the Servant of God became an object of horror; many were astonished at Him.] His face *and* His whole appearance were marred more than any man's, and His form beyond that of the sons of men—but just as many were astonished at Him,
>
> So shall He startle *and* sprinkle many nations, and kings shall shut their mouths because of Him; for that which has not been told them shall they see, and that which they have not heard shall they consider *and* understand.
>
> —ISAIAH 52:14–15 AMPC[18]

For sure, God did not promise we would be free of suffering. But he did promise to give us the peace that surpasses all understanding.

Paul wrote about this peace from prison. His letter to the Philippians is one of joy and hope.

> Let gentleness be seen in every relationship, for our Lord is ever near.
>
> Don't be pulled in different directions or worried about a thing. Be saturated in prayer throughout each day, offering your faith-filled requests before God with overflowing gratitude. Tell him every detail of your life, then God's wonderful peace that transcends human understanding, will make the answers known to you through Jesus Christ. So keep your thoughts continually fixed on all that is authentic and real, honorable and admirable, beautiful and respectful, pure and holy, merciful and kind. And fasten your thoughts on every glorious work of God, praising him always. Follow the example of all that we have imparted to you and the God of peace will be with you in all things.
>
> —PHILIPPIANS 4:5-9 TPT[19]

We won't always receive warnings of oncoming storms. But when we do, we should pay close attention to God's guidance. We can avoid some, but not all, storms. Occasionally we'll pass through a divine tempest meant to strengthen us.[20]

When we fall, regardless of how, where, and why, there's hope. The veil is removed. We have direct access to God who rescues us and who offers life everlasting.

> We can all draw close to him with the veil removed from our faces. And with no veil we all become like mirrors who brightly reflect the glory of the Lord Jesus. We are being transfigured into His very image as we move from one brighter level of glory to

another. And this glorious transfiguration comes from the Lord, who is the Spirit.

—2 CORINTHIANS 3:18 TPT[21]

Remember *this hope* when nights grow long and morning eludes your grasp; when storms rage seemingly without end; when you fall and fear you'll never rise again.

Remember that in your darkest hour, God sees you and knows exactly what you're going through.

When you fall . . .

Draw close to Him.

Draw close to others who love and care about you.

And when you rise . . .

Remember to help others who suffer.

Let your light grow bright.

And let it shine!

APPENDIX

CHRONOLOGICAL ORDER OF CONTENT

Childhood Years: 1985

Chapter 1   Lost in Solon

College Years: 1990-1997

Chapter 2   Unexpected Grace
Chapter 9   The Lens
Chapter 3   The Manifest Presence
Chapter 10   Amtrak Angel

Post College Years: 1999-2003

Chapter 4   Desert Awakening
Chapter 5   A New Home
Chapter 6   Sunday Night Voices
Chapter 11   Information Please!
Chapter 12   Silence!
Chapter 13   Butter Angel
Chapter 14   Drunk in The Park

Professional Years: 2003-2011

Chapter 7   External Voices
Chapter 15   Big Money
Chapter 8   No Ordinary Cat
Chapter 16   When You Fall

NOTES

This section includes all references used throughout the book, including Scripture verses. I have spelled out each Bible version the first time of its use, as in the main body text. Subsequent references are abbreviated.

I have arranged the notes below, according to each chapter, for your reference. And I have chosen sources that I hope the reader will find unique and fun to read, including those that are accessible on the internet.

PREFACE

1. Matthew. 22:51.
2. Freya and Harold Littledale; *Timothy's Forest*, ill., Rosalie Lehrman (New York: Lion Press, 1969).
3. Wikipedia, s.v. "The Chronicles of Narnia," last modified September 16, 2020, 13:40 (UTC), https://en.wikipedia.org/wiki/The_Chronicles_of_Narnia.
4. L. Richard Lessor, *Fuzzies*, ill., Patricia Ellen Ricci (Niles, IL: Argus Communications, 1971).
5. "Learn About Albinism," National Organization for Albinism and Hypopigmentation, accessed September 6, 2018, https://www.albinism.org/learn-about-albinism.

ACKNOWLEDGMENTS

1. 1 Kings 19:12.

CHAPTER 1: LOST IN SOLON

2. Jonathan H. Ellerby, *Inspiration Deficit Disorder: The No-Pill Prescription to End High Stress, Low Energy, and Bad Habits* (Carlsbad, CA: Hay House, Inc., 2010), 166-167. Used by permission of Hay House Publishing, Carlsbad, CA, USA, www.hayhouse.com.

NOTES

3. Gertrude Himmelfarb, *The Roads to Modernity: The British, French, and American Enlightenments* (New York, NY: Vintage Books, 2005).

4. Gertrude Himmelfarb, *The Roads to Modernity: The British, French, and American Enlightenments* (New York, NY: Vintage Books, 2005).

5. Stuart Jeffries, "David Graeber interview: 'So many people spend their working lives doing jobs they think are unnecessary,'" The Guardian, March 21, 2015, https://www.theguardian.com.

    Louise Carpenter, "The Exhaustion Epidemic," *The Guardian*, Dec. 3, 2006, https://www.theguardian.com/lifeandstyle/2006/dec/03/healthandwellbeing.features.

6. Roxane Cohen Silver, E. Alison Holman, Judith Pizarro Andersen, Michael Poulin, Daniel N. McIntosh, and Virginia Gil-Rivas, "Mental- and Physical-Health Effects of Acute Exposure to Media Images of the September 11, 2001, Attacks and the Iraq War," *Psychological Science* 24, no. 9, (Sept. 2013): 1623, doi: 10.1177/0956797612460406.

7. 1 Kings 19:12.

8. Genesis 7:5.

9. Matthew 24:36-38.

10. Jonathan H. Ellerby, *Inspiration Deficit Disorder: The No-Pill Prescription to End High Stress, Low Energy, and Bad Habits* (Carlsbad, CA: Hay House, Inc., 2010), 166-167. Used by permission of Hay House Publishing, Carlsbad, CA, USA, www.hayhouse.com.

CHAPTER 2: UNEXPECTED GRACE

1. Thomas Adams, *The Works of Thomas Adams: Vol. I, Containing Sermons from Text in the Old Testament, &c*, ed. Thomas Smith (Edinburgh: James Nichol, 1861), 61, par. 2, https://miniwebtool.com/roman-numerals-converter/?number=MDCCCLXI.

2. Wikipedia, s.v. "New Formalism," last modified September 12, 2019, 09:11 (UTC), https://en.wikipedia.org/wiki/New_Formalism_(architecture).

3. "Pedestrian Perspective: University at Albany - Uptown Campus," *Albany: The Pedestrian Perspective* (blog), *Blogger*, September 22, 2011, https://urbanalbany.blogspot.com/2011/09/pedestrian-perspective-university-at.html.

NOTES

4. "Learn About Albinism," National Organization for Albinism and Hypopigmentation, accessed September 6, 2018, https://www.albinism.org/learn-about-albinism.

5. "INFJ," Human Metrics, accessed October 18, 2020, http://www.humanmetrics.com/personality/infj.

6. Ashley Boss, "How Meditation Went Mainstream," *Time*, March 9, 2016, https://time.com/4246928/meditation-history-buddhism.

7. "Quadrangle Complex," Institute Archives and Special Collections, Rensselaer Libraries, Rensselaer Polytechnic Institute, accessed September 6, 2019, https://www.rpi.edu/dept/library/html/Archives /buildings.

8. "The Quadrangle - 'Quad,'" Rensselaer Polytechnic Institute, accessed September 6, 2019, http://www.rpi.edu/dept/res-life/html/floorplans-quad.html.

9. Thomas Adams, *The Works of Thomas Adams: Vol. I, Containing Sermons from Text in the Old Testament, &c*, ed. Thomas Smith (Edinburgh: James Nichol, 1861), 61, par. 2, https://miniwebtool.com/roman-numerals-converter/?number=MDCCCLXI.

10. Thomas Adams, *The Works of Thomas Adams: Vol. I, Containing Sermons from Text in the Old Testament, &c*, ed. Thomas Smith (Edinburgh: James Nichol, 1861), 61, par. 2, https://miniwebtool.com/roman-numerals-converter/?number=MDCCCLXI.

CHAPTER 3: THE MANIFEST PRESENCE

1. 2 Corinthians 4:7-9 (*The Passion Translation* [TPT]). Used by permission of Passion & Fire Ministries, Inc., https://www.thepassiontranslation.com.

2. Ravi Zacharias and R. S. B. Sawyer, *Walking from East to West: God in the Shadows* (Grand Rapids: Zondervan, 2006), 218-226. Used by permission of Zondervan, Grand Rapids, MI, USA. https://www.zondervan.com.

3. Dina Spector, "How Long A Person Can Survive Without Water," Independent, February 14, 2006, https://www.independent.co.uk/life-style/health-and-families/health-news/how-long-a-person-can-survive-without-water-a6873341.html.

4. Jane Palmer, "The Creatures That Can Survive Without Water for Years," BBC, September 27, 2016, http://www.bbc.com/earth /story/20160926-the-creatures-that-can-survive-without-water-for-years.

NOTES

5. John 7:38 (TPT). Used by permission of Passion & Fire Ministries, Inc., https://www.thepassiontranslation.com.

6. Acts 2:1-4 (NIV). Used by permission of Biblica, Inc., https://www.biblica.com.

7. Acts 19:1-7 (*Easy-to-Read Version* [ERV]). Used by permission of Bible League International, https://www.bibleleague.org.

8. Joni Eareckson Tada and Steven Estes, *When God Weeps* (Grand Rapids, MI: Zondervan, 1997, 232-240.

9. Philippians 4:10b-13 (TPT). Used by permission of Passion & Fire Ministries, Inc., https://www.thepassiontranslation.com.

10. 2 Corinthians 4:7 (TPT). Used by permission of Passion & Fire Ministries, Inc., https://www.thepassiontranslation.com.

CHAPTER 4: DESERT AWAKENING

1. Josiah Hotchkiss Gilbert and Charles S. Robinson, *Dictionary of Burning Words of Brilliant Writers: A Cyclopedia of Quotations* (New York: Wilbur B. Ketcham, 1895), 400, par. 1. This work is in the public domain. The direct quotation of Alexander Maclaren from p. 400 is in the public domain.

2. 1 Kings 19:12 *(World English Bible* [WEB]).

3. Joshua J. Mark, "Moses," Ancient History Encyclopedia, September 28, 2016, https://www.ancient.eu/Moses.

   Ralph F. Wilson, "Appendix 2. The Route of the Exodus," JesusWalk, accessed September 13, 2019, http://www.jesuswalk.com/moses/appendix_2-route-of-the-exodus.htm.

   Tony Mariot, "How Long Should It Have Taken the Israelites to Get from Egypt to the Promised Land If They Hadn't Gotten Lost?," Quora, April 22, 2019, https://qr.ae/TWKk2C.

4. Matthew 7:7 (WEB).

5. Philippians 4:7 (WEB).

6. Ralph Adolphs. "The Biology of Fear." *Current Biology* 23, no. 2 (January 2013): R79–R93, doi: 10.1016/j.cub.2012.11.055.

7. Roanne Van Voorst, "The Flipside of Fear: Freedom & Desire," Online course module 1.4, Courage Building & Personal Leadership, April 2019.

NOTES

   Used by permission of Hatch, Amsterdam, North Holland, NLD, https://www.iamhatch.com.

8. Wikipedia, s.v. "First Epistle of John," Last modified June 29, 2019, 22:15 (UTC), https://en.wikipedia.org/wiki/First_Epistle_of_John.

9. 1 John 4:18 (NIV). Used by permission of Biblica, Inc., https://www.biblica.com.

10. Bruce D. Schneider, *Energy Leadership* (Hoboken, NJ: John Wiley & Sons, 2008), pp. XV, 11-13.

11. Bruce D. Schneider, *Energy Leadership* (Hoboken, NJ: John Wiley & Sons, 2008), pp. XV, 11-13.

12. Mary Fairchild, "Introduction to 1 Corinthians," Learn Religions, updated May 10, 2019, https://www.learnreligions.com/introduction-to-the-book-of-corinthians-701028.

13. Wikipedia, s.v. "Greek words for love," last modified September 7, 2019, 17:04 (UTC), https://en.wikipedia.org/wiki/Greek_words_for_love.

14. Geoffrey Chaucer, A. Kent Hieatt, and Constance Hieatt, *The Canterbury Tales in Plain and Simple English,* (1964; repr., New York, NY: Bantam Dell, 2006).

15. "The Canterbury Tales: Summary," CliffsNotes, accessed July 26, 2020, https://www.cliffsnotes.com/literature/c/the-canterbury-tales/summary.

16. "The Canterbury Tales: Summary," CliffsNotes, accessed July 26, 2020, https://www.cliffsnotes.com/literature/c/the-canterbury-tales/summary.

17. "The Canterbury Tales: Social Satire," LitCharts, accessed July 26, 2020, https://www.litcharts.com/lit/the-canterbury-tales/themes/social-satire.

18. Wikipedia, s.v. "The Prioress's Tale," last modified June 8, 2020, 06:37 (UTC), https://en.wikipedia.org/wiki/The_Prioress%27s_Tale.

19. Wikipedia, s.v. "The Prioress's Tale," last modified June 8, 2020, 06:37 (UTC), https://en.wikipedia.org/wiki/The_Prioress%27s_Tale.

20. "The Canterbury Tales: The Prioress," LitCharts., accessed July 26, 2020, https://www.litcharts.com/lit/the-canterbury-tales/characters/the-prioress.

21. Galatians 5:22 (TPT).

NOTES

22. "Freedom in The World 2017: Populists and Autocrats: The Dual Threat to Global Democracy," Freedom House, accessed June 8, 2020, https://freedomhouse.org/report /freedom-world/freedom-world-2017.

23. "Freedom in The World 2018: Democracy in Crisis," Freedom House, accessed June 8, 2020, https://freedomhouse.org/report/freedom-world /freedom-world-2018.

24. "Freedom in the World 2020: A Leaderless Struggle for Democracy," Freedom House, accessed August 15, 2020, https:// freedomhouse.org /report/freedom-world/2020/leaderless-struggle-democracy.

25. Dietrich Bonhoeffer, *Life Together: A Discussion of Christian Fellowship*, (1954; repr., New York, NY: HarperOne, 2009), 20, par. 2.

26. Dietrich Bonhoeffer, *Life Together: A Discussion of Christian Fellowship*, (1954; repr., New York, NY: HarperOne, 2009), 20, par. 2.

27. Gilbert and Robinson, *Dictionary of Burning Words of Brilliant Writers*, 400, par. 1. This work is in the public domain. The direct quotation of Alexander Maclaren from p. 400 is in the public domain.

CHAPTER 5: A NEW HOME

1. Richard Feyman, *The Character of Physical Law* (1965; repr., Cambridge, MA: The MIT Press, 2017), 34. Used by permission of The MIT Press. https://mitpress.mit.edu.

2. Wikipedia, s.v. "Solvay, New York," last modified October 1, 2019, 04:51 (UTC), https://en.wikipedia.org/wiki/Solvay,_New _York.

   Wikipedia, s.v. "James Geddes (engineer)," last modified May 2, 2019, 21:02 (UTC), https://en.wikipedia.org/wiki/James_Geddes_(engineer).

3. "Crucible Legacy," Crucible Industries, accessed October 28, 2019, http://www.crucible.com/history.aspx.

4. Rom. 8:28 (TPT). Used by permission of Passion & Fire Ministries, Inc., https://www.thepassiontranslation.com.

5. Ravi Zacharias, *Deliver Us from Evil: Restoring the Soul in a Disintegrating Culture* (Nashville, TN: W. Publishing Group, 1997), 67, par. 5.

6. Job 1:1.

7. Job 1:12.

8. Job 42:12.

NOTES

9. Matthew 27:45-46 (TPT). Used by permission of Passion & Fire Ministries, Inc., https://www.thepassiontranslation.com.

10. Viktor E. Frankl, *Man's Search for Meaning*, (1959; repr., Boston, MA: Beacon Press, 2006), 99.

11. Robert Kegan, "Making Meaning: The Constructive-Developmental Approach to Persons and Practice," *The Personnel and Guidance Journal* 58, no. 5 (1980): 373–380, doi: 10.1002/j.2164-4918.1980.tb00416.x.

    William G. Perry Jr., *Forms of Ethical and Intellectual Development in the College Years: A Scheme* (New York: Holt, Rinehart and Winston, 1970).

12. Neil Postman and Charles Weingartner, *Teaching as a Subversive Activity* (New York, NY: Dell Publishing Co., Inc., 1969).

13. Wikipedia, s.v. "George Kelly (Psychologist)," last modified August 15, 2020, 03:20 (UTC), https://wikipedia.org/wiki/George_Kelly_(Psychologist).

14. Richard G. Tedeschi and Lawrence G. Calhoun, "Posttraumatic Growth: Conceptual Foundations and Empirical Evidence," *Psychological Inquiry* 15, no. 1 (2004): 1-18, doi: 10.1207/s15327965 pli1501_01.

15. P. Alex Linley and Stephen Joseph, "Positive Change Following Trauma and Adversity: A Review," *Journal of Traumatic Stress* 17, no. 1 (2004): 11–21, https://onlinelibrary.wiley.com/doi/10.1023/B%3AJOTS.0000014671.27856.7e.

16. Richard Feyman, *The Character of Physical Law* (1965; repr., Cambridge, MA: The MIT Press, 2017), 34. Used by permission of The MIT Press. https://mitpress.mit.edu.

17. Job 13:15a (NIV). Used by permission of Biblica, Inc., https://www.biblica.com.

18. 1 Kings 19:12 (WEB).

CHAPTER 6: SUNDAY NIGHT VOICES

1. Josiah Hotchkiss Gilbert and Charles S. Robinson, *Dictionary of Burning Words of Brilliant Writers: A Cyclopedia of Quotations* (New York: Wilbur B. Ketcham, 1895), 481. This work is in the public domain. The direct quotation of John Ross Macduff from p. 481 is in the public domain.

2. Mark E. Wilkinson and Khadija S. Shahid, "Proceed with Caution: Low Vision and Driving," *Review of Optometry* 155, no. 4 (April 2018): 74-79.

NOTES

3. Hebrews 11:6 (NIV). Used by permission of Biblica, Inc., https://www.biblica.com.

4. Jessica Timmons, "When Can a Fetus Hear?," Healthline, January 5, 2018, https://www.healthline.com/health/pregnancy/when-can-a-fetus-hear.

5. Alexandra R. Webb, Howard T. Heller, Carol B. Benson, and Amir Lahav, "Mother's Voice and Heartbeat Sounds Elicit Auditory Plasticity in the Human Brain Before Full Gestation," *Proceedings of the National Academy of Sciences of the United States of America*, 112, no. 10 (2015): 3152, doi: 10.1073/pnas.1414924112.

6. Meg Faure, "What Is Bonding and Why Is It Important," Baby Sense, Accessed September 26, 2020, https://www.babysense.com/advice-and-tips/baby/ages-and-stages/mom-and-dad/what-is-bonding-and-why-is-it-important.

7. Regina Sullivan, Rosemarie Perry, Aliza Sloan, Karine Kleinhaus, and Nina Burtchen, "Infant Bonding and Attachment to the Caregiver: Insights from Basic and Clinical Science," *Clinics in Perinatology* 38, no. 4 (2011): 643, doi: 10.1016/j.clp.2011.08.011.

8. Jane Anderson, "The Impact of Family Structure on the Health of Children: Effects of Divorce," *The Linacre Quarterly* 81, no. 4 (2014): 378, doi: 10.1179%2F0024363914Z.00000000087.

9. Heather Sandstrom and Sandra Huerta, *The Negative Effects of Instability on Child Development: A Research Synthesis*, Urban Institute, September 18, 2013, https://www.urban.org/research/publication/negative-effects-instability-child-development-research-synthesis.

10. Christine Courtois, "Dr. Christine Courtois on the Voice and Childhood Trauma: VIDEO," Psychalive, accessed August 1, 2019, https://www.psychalive.org/dr-christine-courtois-on-the-voice-and-childhood-trauma-video.

11. Mark Wolynn, *It Didn't Start with You: How Inherited Family Trauma Shapes Who We Are and How to End the Cycle* (New York: Viking, 2016).

12. Judith Pickering, "Bearing the Unbearable: Ancestral Transmission Through Dreams and Moving Metaphors in the Analytic Field," *The Journal of Analytical Psychology* 57, no. 5 (November 2012): 576-596, doi: 10.1111/j.1468-5922.2012.02004.x.

13. Ephesians 1:5-6 (TPT). Used by permission of Passion & Fire Ministries, Inc., https://www.thepassiontranslation.com.

NOTES

14. Littleton Coin Company, "Ancient Roman Coins: The Roman Republic," accessed August 20, 2020, https://www.littletoncoin.com/shop/Ancient-Roman-Coins.

    Forum Ancient Coins, "Assaria," accessed August 20, 2020, https://www.forumancientcoins.com/numiswiki/view.asp?key=Assaria.

15. Littleton Coin Company, "Guide to Ancient Roman Coinage," accessed August 20, 2020, https://www.littletoncoin.com/shop/DisplayView?storeId=10001&catalogId=29555&eSpotName=LearnNav&staticContent=Guide-to-Ancient-Roman-Coinage.html

16. Bible Gateway, s.v. "Luke 12," accessed August 20, 2020, https://www.biblegateway.com/passage/?search=Luke+12&version=WEB#en-WEB-25466. See footnote b.

17. Jon Kabat-Zinn, *Wherever You Go, There You Are: Mindfulness Meditation in Everyday Life* (New York: Hyperion, 1994).

18. Jon Kabat-Zinn, *Wherever You Go, There You Are: Mindfulness Meditation in Everyday Life* (New York: Hyperion, 1994).

19. Gilbert and Robinson, *Dictionary of Burning Words of Brilliant Writers* (New York, NY: Wilbur B. Ketcham, 1895), 481. This work is in the public domain. The direct quotation of John Ross Macduff from p. 481 is in the public domain.

CHAPTER 7: EXTERNAL VOICES

1. Charles Dickens, *Our Mutual Friend*, (1864-1865; repr., Ware, Hertfordshire, United Kingdom: Wordsworth Editions, 1997), 492.

2. "Clark Reservation State Park," New York State Parks, Recreation and Historic Preservation, accessed November 9, 2019, https://parks.ny.gov/parks/126/details.aspx.

3. "Glacier Lake (Clark Reservation State Park)," New York State Parks, Recreation and Historic Preservation, accessed November 9, 2019, https://www.dec.ny.gov/outdoor/70579.html.

4. Wikipedia, s.v. "Meromictic lake," Last modified September 26, 2019, 06:11 (UTC). https://en.wikipedia.org/wiki/Meromictic_lake.

5. Wikipedia, s.v. "Meromictic lake," Last modified September 26, 2019, 06:11 (UTC). https://en.wikipedia.org/wiki/Meromictic_lake.

NOTES

6. "Plant of the Week: American Hart's Tongue Fern" U.S. Forest Service, accessed November 9, 2019. https://www.fs.fed.us/wildflowers/plant-of-the-week/asplenium_scolopendrium _americanum.shtml.

7. Charles Dickens, *Our Mutual Friend*, (1864-1865; repr., Ware, Hertfordshire, United Kingdom: Wordsworth Editions, 1997), 492.

8. Charles Dickens, *Our Mutual Friend*, (1864-1865; repr., Ware, Hertfordshire, United Kingdom: Wordsworth Editions, 1997), 492.

9. Hebrews 13:1-3 (TPT). Used by permission of Passion & Fire Ministries, Inc., https://www.thepassiontranslation.com.

CHAPTER 8: NO ORDINARY CAT

1. Ron Rhodes, *1001 Unforgettable Quotes About God, Faith, and the Bible* (Eugene, OR: Harvest House Publishers, 2011), 197. The direct quotation of St. Francis of Assisi from p. 197 is in the public domain.

2. "Prophetic Dreams - Definition, Interpretation and Meaning," Dreaming and Sleeping, accessed October 21, 2020, https://dreamingandsleeping.com/prophetic-dreams-definition-interpretation-and-meaning.

3. James S. Grottstein, *Who Is the Dreamer Who Dreams the Dream?: A Study of Psychic Presences* (New York, NY: Routledge, 2009), 15.

4. Oxford Art Online. "Impressionism and Post-Impressionism." Accessed April 29, 2020, https://www.oxfordartonline.com/page/1623.

5. Paul Henley, *The Adventure of the Real: Jean Rouch and the Craft of Ethnographic Cinema* (Chicago, IL: The University of Chicago Press, 2009), 28.

6. Paul Henley, *The Adventure of the Real: Jean Rouch and the Craft of Ethnographic Cinema* (Chicago, IL: The University of Chicago Press, 2009), 28.

7. "Washington's Hidden Underground Station," CGTN America, posted on April 12, 2015, YouTube video, 6:55:00, https://www.youtube.com/watch?v=dfby QnMQpI4, See 6:00.

8. Wikipedia, s.v. "Oneiric (film theory)," last modified December 18, 2019, 18:17 (UTC), https://en.wikipedia.org/wiki/Oneiric_(film_theory).

9. Fariba Bogzaran and Daniel Deslauriers, "A Larger Calling: The Field of Integral Studies," in *Integral Dreaming: A Holistic Approach to Dreams (SUNY series in Dream Studies)* (Albany: State University of New York, 2012), 3-18.

NOTES

10. Joanna Jones, "10 Famous Inventions You Won't Believe Were Inspired by Dreams," accessed July 12, 2020, https://www.viralmojos.com/famous-inventions-inspired-by-dreams.

11. Danny F. Santos, "15 Famous Ideas That Were Invented in Dreams," accessed July 12, 2010, https://www.theclever.com/15-famous-ideas-that-were-invented-in-dreams.

12. Lana Adler, "The Psychology of Altruism: Why Some People Act Selflessly to Help Others, Lana Adler (kalinin1158) (blog), HubPages, December 8, 2015, https://hubpages.com/education/Are-You-Altruistic.

13. Lana Adler, "The Psychology of Altruism: Why Some People Act Selflessly to Help Others, Lana Adler (kalinin1158) (blog), HubPages, December 8, 2015, https://hubpages.com/education/Are-You-Altruistic.

14. Ron Rhodes, *1001 Unforgettable Quotes About God, Faith, and the Bible* (Eugene, OR: Harvest House Publishers, 2011), 197.

15. James S. Grottstein, *Who Is the Dreamer Who Dreams the Dream?: A Study of Psychic Presences* (New York, NY: Routledge, 2009), 15.

16. Ephesians 1:5-6 (TPT). Used by permission of Passion & Fire Ministries, Inc., https://www.thepassiontranslation.com.

CHAPTER 9: THE LENS

1. Eileen Elias Freeman, *Touched by Angels: True Cases of Close Encounters of the Celestial Kind* (New York, NY: Grand Central Publishing, 1994), 71, par. 1. Reprinted by permission of Grand Central Publishing, an imprint of Hachette Book Group, https://www.grandcentralpublishing.com.

2. Eileen Elias Freeman, *Touched by Angels: True Cases of Close Encounters of the Celestial Kind* (New York, NY: Grand Central Publishing, 1994), 71, par. 1. Reprinted by permission of Grand Central Publishing, an imprint of Hachette Book Group, https://www.grandcentralpublishing.com.

3. "What Do Angels Look Like? A Biblical Analysis," What Christians Want to Know, accessed July 7, 2020, https://www.whatchristianswanttoknow.com/what-do-angels-look-like-a-biblical-analysis.

4. Wayne Grudem, "Angels in the Bible: What Do We Actually Know About Them?," Zondervan Academic, December 13, 2017, https://zondervanacademic.com/blog/biblical-facts-angels.

5. The cherubim guarded the entrance to the Garden of Eden. See Genesis 3:24.

NOTES

6. The cherubim accompanied the Ark of the Covenant and the glory of God in the temple. Ezekiel 10:1-21

7. God is enthroned above, between, or among the cherubim. The NIV uses the word "between." The WEB uses "above" and "among." See the following verses in both the NIV and WEB. 1 Samuel 4:4, 2 Samuel 6:2, Isaiah 37:16, Psalm 80:1, and Psalm 99:1.

8. God rides upon the cherubim. See Psalm 18:10.

9. Wayne Grudem, "Angels in the Bible: What Do We Actually Know About Them?," Zondervan Academic, December 13, 2017, https://zondervanacademic.com/blog/biblical-facts-angels.

10. Wayne Grudem, "Angels in the Bible: What Do We Actually Know About Them?," Zondervan Academic, December 13, 2017, https://zondervanacademic.com/blog/biblical-facts-angels.

11. Hope Bolinger, "What Are Archangels in the Bible? How Many Archangels Are There?," July 12, 2019, https://www.christianity.com/wiki/angels-and-demons/what-are-archangels-in-the-bible.html.

    Daniel 10:13 (NIV) Used by permission of Biblica, Inc., https://www.biblica.com.

12. Daniel 10:5-6 (*Amplified Bible* [AMP]). Used by permission of The Lockman Foundation, http://www.lockman.org.

13. "Beryl Gemstone Information," GemSelect, accessed July 7, 2020, https://www.gemselect.com/gem-info/beryl/beryl-info.php.

14. Isaiah 6:1-2 (TPT). Used by permission of Passion & Fire Ministries, Inc., https://www.thepassiontranslation.com.

15. Debbie McDaniel, "5 (Biblical) Reasons Why God Might Send His Angels," Crosswalk, March 17, 2015, https://www.crosswalk.com/faith/spiritual-life/5-biblical-reasons-why-god-might-send-his-angels.html.

16. Psalm 34:7 (TPT). Used by permission of Passion & Fire Ministries, Inc., https://www.thepassiontranslation.com.

17. Hebrews 13:1-3 (TPT). Used by permission of Passion & Fire Ministries, Inc., https://www.thepassiontranslation.com.

18. Mark 11:24. (AMP). Used by permission of The Lockman Foundation, http://www.lockman.org.

19. Colossians 3:1-17.

NOTES

20. 1 John 1:9 (TPT). Used by permission of Passion & Fire Ministries, Inc., https://www.thepassiontranslation.com.

21. Romans 8:1; Isaiah 43:18.

22. Proverbs 16:18.

23. Luke 12:6-7 (TPT). Used by permission of Passion & Fire Ministries, Inc., https://www.thepassiontranslation.com.

CHAPTER 10: AMTRAK ANGEL

1. Isaiah 25:4 (*New Life Version* [NLV]). Used by permission of Barbour Publishing, Inc., https://www.barbourbooks.com.

2. Amtrak, "Old Saybrook, CT (OSB)," Great American Stations, accessed July 2020, https://www.greatamericanstations.com/stations.

3. Forbes West, "Woes of the modern Pharisees," People's World, June 16, 2020, https://www.peoplesworld.org/article/woes-of-the-modern-pharisees-using-the-law-to-oppress-not-uplift.

4. Luke 17:20-21 (*Amplified Bible*, Classic Edition [AMPC]). Used by permission of The Lockman Foundation, http://www.lockman.org.

5. George Eldon Ladd, *A Theology of the New Testament* (Grand Rapids, MI: Wm. B. Eerdmans Publishing Co., 1974), 368, par. 3. Used by permission of Wm. B. Eerdmans Publishing Company, Grand Rapids, MI, USA. www.eerdmans.com.

6. John 1:51 (AMP). Used by permission of The Lockman Foundation, http://www.lockman.org.

7. Philip Wijaya, "What Is the Difference Between Grace and Mercy?," Christianity.com, July 8, 2019, https://www.christianity.com/wiki/christian-terms/what-is-the-difference-between-grace-and-mercy.html.

8. Isaiah 25:4 (*New Life Version* [NLV]). Used by permission of Barbour Publishing, Inc., https://www.barbourbooks.com.

CHAPTER 11: INFORMATION PLEASE!

1. 1 Kings 19:5-7 (ERV). Used by permission of Bible League International, https://www.bibleleague.org.

2. Wikipedia, s.v. "Howard Johnson's," last modified July 24, 2020, 21:29 (UTC), https://en.wikipedia.org/wiki/Howard_Johnson's#cite_note-34.

NOTES

3. 1 Kings 19:5-9 (ERV). Used by permission of Bible League International, bibleleague.org.

4. Bible Hub, "1 Kings: Bible Timeline," accessed August 5, 2020, https://biblehub.com/timeline/1_kings/1.htm.

5. 1 Kings 18:20.

6. Got Questions Ministries, "Why was the worship of Baal and Asherah a constant struggle for the Israelites?," accessed August 5, 2020, https://www.gotquestions.org/Baal-and-Asherah.html.

7. 1 Kings 18:20-24.

8. 1 Kings 18:25-39.

9. 1 Kings 18:40.

10. 1 Kings 18:45; 19:1.

11. Jim Robidoux, "The Story of the Prophet Elijah, Jezebel and King Ahab," Manchester Ink Link, November 11, 2018, https://manchesterinklink.com/the-story-of-the-prophet-elijah-jezebel-and-king-ahab.

12. 1 Kings 19:2.

13. 1 Kings 19:3-4a.

14. 1 Kings 19:4; 9b-10.

15. 1 Kings 19:5-7 (ERV). Used by permission of Bible League International, https://www.bibleleague.org.

16. Josiah Hotchkiss Gilbert and Charles S. Robinson, *Dictionary of Burning Words of Brilliant Writers: A Cyclopedia of Quotations* (New York, NY: Wilbur B. Ketcham, 1895), 428. This work is in the public domain. The direct quotation of Henry Ecob from p. 428 is in the public domain.

17. Jonathan Lipnick, "What is The Holy of Holies?," Israel Institute of Biblical Studies, January 10, 2017, https://blog.israelbiblicalstudies.com/holy-land-studies/what-was-the-holy-of-holies.

18. Charles Bumgardner, "The Thickness of the Temple Veil," Orchard Keeper, April 6, 2010, https://cbumgardner.wordpress.com/2010/04/06/the-thickness-of-the-temple-veil.

    Jack Wellman, "Tearing of the Temple Curtain," accessed August 8, 2020, https://www.whatchristianswanttoknow.com/tearing-of-the-temple-curtain-why-was-this-significant.

NOTES

19. *The Veil Removed*, directed by Branden J. Stanley (Chicago, IL: Spirit Juice Studios, 2019), https://www.spiritjuicestudios.com. See also https://theveilremoved.com.

20. *It's a Miracle*, season 2, episode 10, "Thanksgiving Blessing," directed by Adam Briles and Ron Brody, aired January 1, 1999, on PAX TV, https://www.amazon.com/gp/video/detail/B0721B2NTS/ref=atv_dp_season_select_atf.

    Questar Entertainment, "Dinner with an Angel - It's a Miracle," uploaded July 11, 2019, YouTube video, 7:48, https://www.youtube.com/watch?v=s6BTvsQbWxw.

CHAPTER 12: SILENCE!

1. Proverbs 13:17 (*The Voice* [VOICE]). Used by permission of Thomas Nelson, Inc. and Ecclesia Bible Society, https://www.thomasnelson.com.

2. Proverbs 13:17 (*The Voice* [VOICE]). Used by permission of Thomas Nelson, Inc. and Ecclesia Bible Society, https://www.thomasnelson.com.

3. Matthew 5:9 (AMP). Used by permission of The Lockman Foundation, http://www.lockman.org.

4. Charles R. Swindoll, "2 Timothy: Paul's Swan Song, Part 1," August 21 to October 16, 2017, Insight for Living Ministries, audio file, 26:51, https://insight.org/broadcasts/player/?bid=1479&ga=bible_pages&start=25.

5. Christine DiGiacomo, "Why did Paul write to Timothy?," *Growing Relationships with Jesus and Others* (blog), *All About GOD*, October 4, 2013, http://www.allaboutgod.net/profiles/blogs/why-did-paul-write-to-timothy.

6. Proverbs 24:15-16 (TPT). Used by permission of Passion & Fire Ministries, Inc., https://www.thepassiontranslation.com.

7. Proverbs 11:14 (AMPC). Used by permission of The Lockman Foundation, http://www.lockman.org.

8. Galatians 6:2 (AMP). Used by permission of The Lockman Foundation, http://www.lockman.org.

9. Exodus 10:5 (VOICE). Used by permission of Thomas Nelson, Inc. and Ecclesia Bible Society, https://www.thomasnelson.com.

NOTES

10. Isaiah 44.3 (TPT). Used by permission of Passion & Fire Ministries, Inc., https://www.thepassiontranslation.com.
11. Isaiah 59:21 (TPT). Used by permission of Passion & Fire Ministries, Inc., https://www.thepassiontranslation.com.
12. Proverbs 3:27 (NIV). Used by permission of Biblica, Inc., https://www.biblica.com.
13. Romans 15:1 (VOICE). Used by permission of Thomas Nelson, Inc. and Ecclesia Bible Society, https://www.thomasnelson.com.
14. Matthew 18:19 (AMPC). Used by permission of The Lockman Foundation, http://www.lockman.org.

CHAPTER 13: BUTTER ANGEL

1. Eileen Elias Freeman, *Touched by Angels: True Cases of Close Encounters of the Celestial Kind* (New York, NY: Grand Central Publishing, 1994), 71, par. 1. Reprinted by permission of Grand Central Publishing, an imprint of Hachette Book Group, https://www.grandcentralpublishing.com.
2. Isaiah 7:14-15 (AMPC). Used by permission of The Lockman Foundation, http://www.lockman.org.
3. Rick Nauert, "Infants Understand Concept of Fairness," Psych Central, August 8, 2018, https://psychcentral.com/news/2012/02/20/infants-understand-concept-of-fairness/35049.html.
4. April Fox, "When Do Babies Stop Jar Food?," Healthfully, June 13, 2017, https://healthfully.com/219387-4-month-baby-diet.html.
5. John 16:33 (NIV). Used by permission of Biblica, Inc., https://www.biblica.com.
6. John 16:33 (TPT). Used by permission of Passion & Fire Ministries, Inc., https://www.thepassiontranslation.com.

CHAPTER 14: DRUNK IN THE PARK

1. Proverbs 11:2 (AMP). Used by permission of The Lockman Foundation, http://www.lockman.org.
2. Dicitionary.com, s.v. "Humble," accessed September 4, 2020, https://www.dictionary.com/browse/humble.

NOTES

3. Wikipedia, s.v. "Humility," last modified August 18, 2020, 07:54 (UTC), https://en.wikipedia.org/wiki/Humility.
4. Proverbs 11:2 (TPT). Used by permission of Passion & Fire Ministries, Inc., https://www.thepassiontranslation.com.
5. Proverbs 11:2 (NIV). Used by permission of Biblica, Inc., https://www.biblica.com.
6. Proverbs 11:2 (VOICE). Used by permission of Thomas Nelson, Inc. and Ecclesia Bible Society, https://www.thomasnelson.com.
7. Proverbs 3:5-6 (NIV). Used by permission of Biblica, Inc., https://www.biblica.com.
8. Proverbs 22:4 (NIV). Used by permission of Biblica, Inc., https://www.biblica.com.
9. Proverbs 22:4 (AMP). Used by permission of The Lockman Foundation, http://www.lockman.org.
10. Luke 17:20-21 (AMPC).
11. Matthew 12:2b (TPT). Used by permission of Passion & Fire Ministries, Inc., https://www.thepassiontranslation.com.
12. Matthew 12:3-9 (TPT). Used by permission of Passion & Fire Ministries, Inc., https://www.thepassiontranslation.com.
13. Matthew 5:20 (TPT). Used by permission of Passion & Fire Ministries, Inc., https://www.thepassiontranslation.com.
14. Matthew 18:3 (NIV). Used by permission of Biblica, Inc., https://www.biblica.com.
15. John 10:27 (VOICE). Used by permission of Thomas Nelson, Inc. and Ecclesia Bible Society, https://www.thomasnelson.com.
16. Romans 1:17 (TPT). Used by permission of Passion & Fire Ministries, Inc., https://www.thepassiontranslation.com.
17. John 20:25b (NIV). Used by permission of Biblica, Inc., https://www.biblica.com.
18. John 20:26 (TPT). Used by permission of Passion & Fire Ministries, Inc., https://www.thepassiontranslation.com.
19. John 20:27-28 (TPT). Used by permission of Passion & Fire Ministries, Inc., https://www.thepassiontranslation.com.

NOTES

20. John 20:29 (TPT). Used by permission of Passion & Fire Ministries, Inc., https://www.thepassiontranslation.com.

21. Hebrews 13:1-3 (TPT). Used by permission of Passion & Fire Ministries, Inc., https://www.thepassiontranslation.com.

CHAPTER 15: BIG MONEY

1. Marcus Tullius Cicero, *On Duties, 44 B.C.*, trans. Walter Miller (Cambridge, MA: Harvard University Press, 1913), 43. This work and the direct quotation of Cicero from p. 43 are in the public domain.

2. Marcus Tullius Cicero, *On Duties, 44 B.C.*, trans. Walter Miller (Cambridge, MA: Harvard University Press, 1913), 43.

3. Dictionary.com, s.v. "Blessing," accessed September 7, 2020, https://www.dictionary.com/browse/blessing.

4. Dictionary.com, s.v. "Abundance," accessed September 7, 2020, https://www.dictionary.com/browse/abundance.

5. Wikipedia, s.v. "Value theory," last modified July 22, 2020, 17:00 (UTC), https://en.wikipedia.org/wiki/Value_theory.

6. Wikipedia, s.v. "Ethics," last modified September 27, 2020, 07:41 (UTC), https://en.wikipedia.org/wiki/Ethics.

7. Wikipedia, s.v. "Life Stance," last modified February 27, 2020, 15:45 (UTC), https://en.wikipedia.org/wiki/Life_stance.

8. Wikipedia, s.v. "Intrinsic value (ethics)," last modified August 6, 2020, 00:31 (UTC), https://en.wikipedia.org/wiki/Intrinsic_value_(ethics).

9. Luke Nix, "Do Humans Have Intrinsic Value?," CrossExamined.org, September 28, 2019, https://crossexamined.org/do-humans-have-intrinsic-value.

10. Wikipedia, s.v. "Intrinsic value (animal ethics)," last modified August 13, 2020, UTC (17:02), https://en.wikipedia.org/wiki/Intrinsic_value_(animal_ethics).

11. Genesis 1:27 (AMP). Used by permission of The Lockman Foundation, http://www.lockman.org.

12. James 1:17 (TPT). Used by permission of Passion & Fire Ministries, Inc., https://www.thepassiontranslation.com.

13. Mark 8:38 (TPT). Used by permission of Passion & Fire Ministries, Inc., https://www.thepassiontranslation.com.

NOTES

14. Mark 16:10 (TPT).
15. Mark 16:1 (TPT). Used by permission of Passion & Fire Ministries, Inc., https://www.thepassiontranslation.com.
16. Proverbs 17:3 (TPT). Used by permission of Passion & Fire Ministries, Inc., https://www.thepassiontranslation.com.
17. 2 Corinthians 9:6 (NIV). Used by permission of Biblica, Inc., https://www.biblica.com.
18. 2 Corinthians 9:10 (NIV). Used by permission of Biblica, Inc., https://www.biblica.com.
19. Phillips Brooks, "The Gift and Its Return," in *Sermons Preached in English Churches* (New York, NY: E. P. Dutton & Company, 1883), 268-287.
20. Brian Tracy, "Using the Law of Reciprocity and Other Persuasion Techniques Correctly," posted on January 29, 2015, YouTube video, 5:58:00, https://youtu.be/n1zNwA61Y7g.
21. Luke 6:28 (TPT). Used by permission of Passion & Fire Ministries, Inc., https://www.thepassiontranslation.com.
22. Marcus Tullius Cicero, *On Duties, 44 B.C.*, trans. Walter Miller (Cambridge, MA: Harvard University Press, 1913), 43.
23. Luke 6:38 (NIV). Used by permission of Biblica, Inc., https://www.biblica.com.

CHAPTER 16: WHEN YOU FALL

1. Psalm 145:14 (VOICE). Used by permission of Thomas Nelson, Inc. and Ecclesia Bible Society, https://www.thomasnelson.com.
2. Camille Moore, "15 of the Toughest Neighborhoods in Philadelphia," Housely.com, 2015, accessed September 9, 2020, https://housely.com/15-toughest-neighborhoods-philadelphia.
3. Sam Sparkes, "The 10 Worst Neighborhoods in Philadelphia for 2020," RoadSnakcs.com, February 26, 2020, https://www.roadsnacks.net/worst-philadelphia-neighborhoods.
4. John 16:33 (AMPC). Used by permission of The Lockman Foundation, http://www.lockman.org.
5. Psalm 145:14 (VOICE). Used by permission of Thomas Nelson, Inc. and Ecclesia Bible Society, https://www.thomasnelson.com.

NOTES

6. David Peach, "Examples of Trials in the Bible: 7 Biblical Stories," What Christians Want to Know, accessed September 12, 2020, https://www.what christianswanttoknow.com/examples-of-trials-in-the-bible-7-biblical -stories.

7. David Peach, "Examples of Trials in the Bible: 7 Biblical Stories," What Christians Want to Know, accessed September 12, 2020, https://www.what christianswanttoknow.com/examples-of-trials-in-the-bible-7-biblical -stories.

8. David Peach, "Examples of Trials in the Bible: 7 Biblical Stories," What Christians Want to Know, accessed September 12, 2020, https://www.what christianswanttoknow.com/examples-of-trials-in-the-bible-7-biblical -stories.

9. David Peach, "Examples of Trials in the Bible: 7 Biblical Stories," What Christians Want to Know, accessed September 12, 2020, https://www.what christianswanttoknow.com/examples-of-trials-in-the-bible-7-biblical -stories.

10. David Peach, "Examples of Trials in the Bible: 7 Biblical Stories," What Christians Want to Know, accessed September 12, 2020, https://www.what christianswanttoknow.com/examples-of-trials-in-the-bible-7-biblical -stories.

11. David Peach, "Examples of Trials in the Bible: 7 Biblical Stories," What Christians Want to Know, accessed September 12, 2020, https://www.what christianswanttoknow.com/examples-of-trials-in-the-bible-7-biblical -stories.

12. George Lawson, "David's Afflictions and Fears," Bible Hub, accessed September 12, 2020, https://biblehub.com/sermons/auth/lawson/david %27s_afflictions_and_fears.htm.

13. "How Many Psalms Did David Write?," Got Questions Ministries, accessed September 12, 2020, https://www.gotquestions.org/Psalms-David.html.

14. Matthew 12:40.

15. Daniel chapter 6.

16. Daniel chapter 3.

17. Kenneth Kimutai Too, "Who Were the Twelve Disciples (Apostles) Of Jesus?," April 25, 2017, WorldAtlas, https://www.worldatlas.com/articles /who-were-the-twelve-disciples-apostles-of-jesus.html.

NOTES

"Do You Know How the 13 Apostles Died?," Bible One, accessed September 12, 2020, http://www.bibleone.net/apostles.htm.

Walter E. Gast, "Emblems of the Apostles," Symbols in Christian Art & Architecture, Copyright 2000, Accessed September 13, 2020, http://www.planetgast.net/symbols/apostles/apostles.html.

Christine DiGiacomo, "Why did Paul write to Timothy?," *Growing Relationships with Jesus and Others* (blog), *All About GOD*, October 4, 2013, http://www.allaboutgod.net/profiles/blogs/why-did-paul-write-to-timothy.

Wikipedia, s.v. "Simon the Zealot," last modified September 2, 2020, 15:09 (UTC), https://en.wikipedia.org/wiki/Simon_the_Zealot.

Earnest A. Wallis Budge, ed., "Chapter XXXII: Of the Death of The Prophets; How They Died, and (Where) Each One of Them Was Buried," in *The Book of the Bee* (Oxford: United Kingdom, The Clarendon Press, 1886).

"How Did Judas Die?," Got Questions Ministries, accessed September 12, 2020, https://www.gotquestions.org/Judas-die.html.

18. Isaiah 52:14-15 (AMPC). Used by permission of The Lockman Foundation, http://www.lockman.org.

19. Philippians 4:5-9 (TPT). Used by permission of Passion & Fire Ministries, Inc., https://www.thepassiontranslation.com.

20. David E. Schoen, *Divine Tempest: The Hurricane as a Psychic Phenomenon* (Toronto, ON, Inner City Books, 1998).

21. 2 Corinthians 3:18 (TPT). Used by permission of Passion & Fire Ministries, Inc., https://www.thepassiontranslation.com.

ABOUT THE AUTHOR

JASON SIGNOR IS a social worker, counselor, and life coach. He is the founder of Your Amazing Journey, a coaching service that helps people with disabilities navigate career change.

A graduate of the University at Buffalo (MSW) and Institute of Professional Excellence in Coaching (iPEC) in 2018, International Association of Trauma Professionals in 2013, and Syracuse University in 2007 (M.S.), Jason has studied and worked in the human services for two decades.

He completed his undergraduate degree in music at Syracuse University where he studied saxophone and composition. And he studied the Art and Technology of Perfumery through PerfumersWorld in Thailand.

Jason's new book, *From Beyond the Veil*, about his spiritual journey, combines creative and research writing styles, and reflects his extensive experience in the human services and arts.

Jason is a lover of God, social research, the arts, and animals—especially cats. He is an identical twin. He grew up in Cortland, New York, USA and now lives in Amherst, New York. This is his first published book.

ABOUT THE TYPE

THE BODY FONT of this book is Janson Text. Janson is a set of serif typefaces that originated in the Dutch Baroque era, created by Miklós (Nicholas) Tótfalusi Kis (1650–1702), a Hungarian-Transylvanian schoolmaster, punch-cutter, and Protestant pastor.[1]

Kis developed a liking for printing—and created the Janson typeface—after he helped print a Hungarian Protestant translation of the Bible in Amsterdam.

The typeface draws its name from Anton Janson (1620–1687), a Leipzig-based printer and punch-cutter from the Netherlands.

The crisp, moderately-high-contrast font is a popular for body copy. Its modern applications include *Architectural Digest* and *Philosophy Now* in the United States, and *Journal of the Printing Historical Society* in the United Kingdom.

---

[1] Wikipedia, s.v. "Janson," last modified August 28, 2020, 16:34 (UTC), https://en.wikipedia.org/wiki/Janson.

ABOUT THE COVER

THE CREATOR OF the book's cover is Joshua Holmes, an author, editor, fine artist, and graphic designer based in York, Pennsylvania. To view Josh's work or to contact him visit http://www.jahbookdesign.com.

The cover photo is of Valley of the Gods in southeastern Utah, United states. It is a popular setting for western movies, commercials, and television shows including CBS's *Airwolf* (1984-1987) and two episodes of BBC's Doctor Who—"The Impossible Astronaut" and "Day of the Moon"—aired in 2011.[1]

The cover depicts the hand of God pulling back a veil to reveal the beautiful vista of the Valley of the Gods, an intentional allegory to the tearing of the temple veil in Biblical times that symbolized Jesus's death and resurrection, opening the way to salvation for all.

---

[1] Wikipedia, s.v. "Valley of the Gods," last updated august 31, 2020, 17:02 (UTC), https://en.wikipedia.org/wiki/Valley_of_the_Gods; "Valley of the Gods," Utah.com, accessed November 10, 2020, https://utah.com/monument-valley/valley-of-the-gods.

LET'S CONNECT!

CONNECT WITH THE author and other readers on Facebook and Instagram. Discuss the book, ask questions, share your thoughts and stories! To explore life and career coaching opportunities offered by the author, visit Your Amazing Journey!

Facebook

https://www.facebook.com/groups/frombeyondtheveil

Instagram

https://www.instagram.com/from_beyond_the_veil

Your Amazing Journey

https://jasonsignor.net

Made in the USA
Columbia, SC
14 December 2020